A TOLERANT COUNTRY?

Colin Holmes is Professor of History at the University of Sheffield. He has written widely on the history of immigration and minority groups. His publications include: *Immigrants and Minorities in British Society* (1978); *Anti-Semitism in British Society 1876–1939* (1979) and *John Bull's Island. Immigration and British Society 1871–1971* (1988). He is also joint editor of the journal *Immigrants and Minorities*.

in the same series

Wealth and Inequality in Britain
W. D. Rubinstein

The Government of Space
Alison Ravetz

Educational Opportunity and Social Change in England
Michael Sanderson

A Property-owning Democracy?
M. J. Daunton

Sport in Britain
Tony Mason

The Labour Movement in Britain
John Saville

The Voluntary Impulse
Frank Prochaska

British Welfare Policy
Anne Digby

No Alternative? Unemployment in Britain
Sean Glynn

Judicial Punishment in England
J. A. Sharpe

Bad Times: Unemployment in British Social and Political History
Noel Whiteside

A TOLERANT COUNTRY?

*Immigrants, Refugees
and Minorities in Britain*

Colin Holmes

faber and faber
LONDON · BOSTON

First published in 1991
by Faber and Faber Limited
3 Queen Square London WC1N 3AU

Photoset by Parker Typesetting Service Leicester
Printed in Great Britain by
Clays Ltd St Ives plc

A CIP record for this book is available from the British Library

ISBN 0-571-15426-3

Series Editors:
Avner Offer – University of York
F. M. L. Thompson – Institute of Historical Research,
University of London

It is widely recognized that many of the problems of present-day society are deeply rooted in the past, but the actual lines of historical development are often known only to a few specialists, while the policy-makers and analysts themselves frequently rely on a simplified, dramatized, and misleading version of history. Just as the urban landscape of today was largely built in a world that is no longer familiar, so the policy landscape is shaped by attitudes and institutions formed under very different conditions in the past. This series of specially commissioned handbooks aims to provide short, up-to-date studies in the evolution of current problems, not in the form of narratives but as critical accounts of the ways in which the present is formed by the past, and of the roots of present discontents. Designed for those with little time for extensive reading in the specialized literature, the books contain full bibliographies for further study. The authors aim to be as accurate and comprehensive as possible, but not anodyne; their arguments, forcefully expressed, make the historical experience available in challenging form, but do not presume to offer ready-made solutions.

Contents

Preface

A Tolerant Country? reflects my interest in the responses encountered by immigrants, refugees and minorities in Britain.

In a brief monograph it is possible to concentrate on only a limited number of themes and I have dwelt upon those issues and developments which are of particular interest to me. The format of the Faber Historical Handbooks requires that the book is written with the intelligent general reader in view, but I hope it will circulate also among a more specialized audience. The books in the series are traditionally light in footnotes: such notes appear essentially for the purpose of identifying quotations. A reader wishing to pursue any of my themes in greater detail will be assisted by the working bibliography.

I drew a line under my reading for the book in the opening days of 1990. The perceptive reader will recognize one or two passing comments of topical significance which were inserted after that date. Such are the trials of writing contemporary history.

In the course of producing the book I have incurred a number of debts. My thanks go in particular to Tony Kushner, Kenny Lunn, David Mayall and Panikos Panayi, four members of the 'Sheffield School' specializing in the history of immigration and minorities. Each has offered sound advice: none is responsible for the final draft. Avner Offer and Michael Thompson, the joint editors of Historical Handbooks, also advanced their opinions. Faber and Faber waited patiently for the final version. Valerie Heap typed my text into a finished state, aided by the ever-dependable Susan Sharman and Maveen Smallman. Finally, my family, to whom I am once again indebted, created the space in which, eventually, I could bring the project to fruition.

Colin Holmes
Sheffield

I

Contemporary issues

Few people in Britain can be unaware of the process of immigration which the country has experienced since the end of the Second World War. However, not many historians have displayed any interest in this development or indeed in the longer chain of immigration into Britain. This neglect has embraced not only immigrant newcomers who for economic, social or cultural reasons, or a mixture of such influences, left their native countries for a temporary or permanent stay in Britain. Refugees who sought shelter on account of racial, religious or political persecution have also been neglected. The result is that anyone who turns to standard histories of Britain finds immigration, and the hopes, aims and aspirations of the individuals caught up in it, reduced to passing incidental comments, relegated to the footnotes or, more seriously, totally ignored, consigned for ever into historical darkness.

It is not only immigrants and refugees who have been marginalized or obliterated in this fashion. The history of many minority groups, characterized by a sense of group consciousness, who can trace their origins to immigration, whether directly or through descent, has also been widely ignored. If the descendants of immigrants from the Caribbean and the Indian sub-continent who came to Britain after the Second World War have received searching, sometimes obsessive, attention from social scientists, little interest has been shown in the history of these minorities. In the case of some other groups the silence is total. There is no general study of the Irish in Britain which carries comprehensive detail on the second and third generations of Irish descent. The Polish-descended minority has been similarly ignored. Any historian enquiring whether Britain has been remarkable for its toleration towards immigrants, refugees and the minorities related to these groups needs to recognize how many pieces are still missing from the overall historical jigsaw.

The bulk of the evidence deployed here is therefore drawn from the experiences of the first-generation immigrants and refugees, and in examining responses towards these groups a wide sweep of recent history is covered. A useful starting point for any such enquiry is 1871, in other words, one hundred years before the important 1971 Immigration Act. Before embarking on this survey, however, it is important to set the scene by examining contemporary developments, concentrating on the years since 1979, the period of Thatcherism.

In contrast to the relative neglect of groups such as the Hong Kong Chinese, Chilean exiles, the 'boat people' of Vietnam, the Tamils from Sri Lanka, unauthorized immigrant workers from the Philippines and Latin America, as well as various Europeans, abundant contemporary material, though of sharply varying quality, is available on Blacks (those of Afro-Caribbean descent), and also on Asians deriving from the Indian sub-continent. It is upon these Blacks and Asians that attention is focussed initially. No attempt is made to recover the full range of their recent past: the enquiry concentrates on whether or not the groups have been tolerated.

The question is important, since an emphasis on toleration, which is usually related to the tradition of liberty, finds its way into official and semi-official enquiries and features prominently in the pronouncements of public figures, as well as in popular discourse. The claim is not that Blacks and Asians have been warmly embraced in Britain or that they have been viewed with indifference. It is more specific. It is that these groups have been positively and voluntarily endured and that a pronounced degree of self-restraint has been evident in the responses they have encountered. Fired by this belief, the survey *Colour and Citizenship* which some of its compilers regarded as a Royal Commission on immigration, attempted in 1969 to demonstrate that during the years of primary immigration from the Caribbean and the Indian sub-continent, British society had revealed its characteristically tolerant face to the newcomers. Survey data emphasized that 35 per cent of the survey sample were 'almost or entirely free of prejudice'.[1] Since 'people are asked to make abstract choices in imaginary situations',[2] such surveys must be treated with caution. Even without this important qualification, the details in *Colour and Citizenship* are open to differing interpretations. One is reminded that there are three types of lies. However, it is socially significant that the compilers of the data leaned towards an interpretation which promoted a public celebration of Britain as a tolerant country.

Other recent survey evidence, although possessing a more complex structure, also reflects the strength of the tolerant tradition. An analysis of social attitudes carried out in 1984 revealed that 90 per cent of the survey sample believed that Blacks and Asians in Britain met with prejudice. However, 64 per cent of the respondents placed themselves in the 'not prejudiced at all' category and only 4 per cent admitted to being 'very prejudiced'.[3] Hostility is regarded as the property of others; it is difficult to admit to its possession oneself, in a culture which prides itself on the strength of its toleration.

Before considering responses towards Blacks and Asians a preliminary task is to delineate the major contours of these minorities. The latest available survey, released in July 1990 and relating to the years 1986 to 1988, suggests an average population of Blacks and Asians of 1.93 million. This figure includes immigrants from the Caribbean and the Indian sub-continent but also incorporates those people of Black or Asian descent who have been born in Britain. From the 1970s these British-born groups begin to assume a greater numerical and social significance. In total, the Asian groups outnumbered the Blacks and were growing at a faster rate, with fertility levels for women born on the Indian sub-continent higher than the levels of their British-born contemporaries. The Indians – calculated at 787,000 – constituted the largest self-identified Asian group. In order to secure a sense of perspective, the figure of 1.93 million for the combined Black and Asian minorities needs to be set against a total population in Great Britain of about 54.51 million. It also deserves to be recognized that the majority of immigrants and refugees who came to Britain after 1945 were white. The frequent stress on Britain as a multi-racial society is apt to obscure this point.

Nevertheless, by the 1980s, Blacks and Asians had become more numerous than at any other time in their history in Britain.

By this time other discernible changes had already occurred. Significant spatial developments had taken place. Blacks and Asians no longer remained confined to the capital, the ports and a number of university towns, as they had essentially been in 1945. Their new place lay in the great conurbations. During these years a marked diversification in occupational structure and a greater involvement in public life can also be traced. This increased public salience had become evident at parliamentary level, consequent upon the return, in the 1987 general election, of Diane Abbott, Paul Boateng, Bernie Grant and Keith Vaz, as well as in local government, and in official organizations, particularly in the so-called 'race relations industry'. In addition, a continuing visibility persisted in sport and a heightened presence had developed in cultural life, particularly in music and literature.

Nevertheless, even amid this increased prominence, many Blacks and Asians remained firmly locked into working-class structures, employed in types of work which remained particularly sensitive to downswings in the economy, and confined in their residence to inner-city areas with decaying infrastructures and serious economic and social problems which the policies of successive governments had failed to overcome. Furthermore, before we become self-satisfied regarding the liberal openness of British society, and possibly nourishing the belief that over the longer term all problems will evaporate, another degree of qualification is necessary. Success in business and certain professions – more evident in the case of Asians than Blacks – could be regarded as a form of compensation achieved through self-employment for the injustice of racial discrimination practised by employers. It is significant that one of the Black QCs on the list of new silks announced by the Lord Chancellor's Department in 1988 said that, in career terms, this leap into legal independence was 'the only option open to me'.[4] His emphasis is a firm reminder that career success and its related benefits cannot always be totally divorced from white hostility. On that note a start can now be made on an extended consideration of white responses.

When the Conservatives were returned to power in 1979 Blacks

and Asians had to contend with a government which was particularly committed in its economic policy to restoring the profitability of British capitalism and at the same time putting organized
labour in its place. Hence the interest in trade union legislation. But
the Conservatives also possessed a populist dimension which
stressed the need to put Britain first. While the Government's
economic policy could affect Blacks and Asians as workers, its
populism, which could easily be interpreted as 'white Britain first',
posed other potential dangers. This sense of possible vulnerability
also emerges from a reading of the Conservative Party's 1979
election manifesto which, in line with its appeal to anti-immigrant
voters, promised to introduce a number of policy initiatives
relating to immigration and race relations.

But how, in practice, did Conservative policy develop once the
party returned to power? One logical starting point in any such
enquiry relates to conditions of entry. Immigration from the Commonwealth started to be controlled by the British Government in
1962 and various measures of the 1960s were followed by a piece of
'fine tuning'[5] in the 1971 Immigration Act. Notwithstanding the
strict controls established by the 1971 Act, and a later tightening of
the related immigration rules, a new bill intended to stiffen the
system still further was introduced in November 1987. When this
piece of legislation came into force in August 1988 a number of new
restrictions entered the statute-book. The Act required male Commonwealth citizens to show that they could maintain and accommodate their families without recourse to public funds. It forbade
the entry of second wives of polygamous marriages. The new
legislation also made overstaying a criminal offence. In addition, it
limited the right of appeal of those people who had lived in the
country for less than seven years and who were being deported for
overstaying or for a breach of the conditions attaching to their
residence in Britain.

In defence of this fresh legislation the Home Secretary
emphasized that the recommendations to tighten the provisions of
the 1971 Act signalled the Government's 'realistic' approach to
immigration control.[6] The legislation testified to more than that.
The measure simultaneously reflected and reinforced popular
opinion; indeed, certain voices still sounded in the 1980s urging the

necessity, not merely of control, but also of repatriation. Taken together with the May 1987 Immigration (Carriers' Liability) Act, as a result of which airline and shipping companies bringing to the United Kingdom people who had no right of entry faced fines of up to £1,000 for each offence, the 1988 Immigration Act strengthened official powers over entry and deportation. These measures of the late 1980s need to be viewed against the earlier British Nationality Act of 1981 in which British citizenship, which provided a guarantee of unrestricted entry into the United Kingdom, enshrined in citizenship law the subtle racial discrimination already present in immigration legislation. It is clear that stricter immigration control, rather than any strengthening of the 1976 Race Relations Act or other actions against racial discrimination, remained at the centre of Conservative policy throughout the 1980s.

The Home Secretary had justified the new immigration legislation in part by claiming that it would assist the cause of racial harmony in Britain's cities, a line of reasoning which had been employed since the early days of immigration control to justify the system of restrictive entry. Notwithstanding the increasingly strict legislation which had already been placed on the statute-book, evidence from the 1980s suggests that considerable opposition still remained towards immigrants from the Caribbean and the Indian sub-continent and more generally towards Black and Asian groups. Why the Government believed that even tighter legislation, which helped to perpetuate the image of Blacks and Asians as 'problem groups', would produce any greater harmony in the future is not without interest. Rather than pursue that particular question, however, the claim that considerable opposition towards Blacks and Asians continued to swirl in Britain in the 1980s needs to be substantiated.

Some opposition towards immigrants, refugees and minorities can be related to the processes of the individual personality. This form of enmity can be defined as prejudice. But the majority of opposition is socially and culturally generated, rather than organically related to the individual psyche. This latter form of hostility can be described as antipathy. In the 1980s in some sections of the press antipathetic sentiment towards Blacks and Asians appeared in the form of a daily dose. In other instances it assumed a more subtle garb through the gratuitous insertion of adjectives such as 'Black' or 'coloured', a device frequently employed in reports of criminal activity.

Hostile comment also filtered into the currency of everyday talk in areas where Black and Asian communities had been formed. Hence an old man in Bradford in an undisguised 'spasm of hatred' directed against Pakistanis, exploded with the observation, 'Contaminating the country, that's what they're doing – contaminating us all! We all think they're horrible – no one likes 'em. Live on filth they do – take my advice and keep well away – catch anything off them you could'.[7] Hostile sentiment also stretched into Parliament where concern could be expressed, albeit in more sophisticated terms than in working-class Bradford, about the undesirable importation of 'tribes and cultures'[8] and the social danger to British society which allegedly followed upon the injection of such standards.

At certain times hostility moved from thought to action. One graphic example occurred in the stand taken in 1987 by some white parents in Dewsbury who objected to their children being educated in a school attended predominantly by Asian children whose families had come to Britain from the Indian sub-continent. This development triggered in part by the opting-out proposals in the Education Bill, led in the autumn of 1988 to the withdrawal of the white children to another school. A later case, resolved in the spring of 1990, resulted in a ruling by the Secretary of State for Education that parents may select their children's school on racial grounds and that this preference stood above the requirements of race relations legislation. These conflicts reflected essentially a cultural clash which assumed racial overtones. It had been present in earlier years and remained ripe at all times for political exploitation.

The clash of cultures also loomed large in the so-called Rushdie affair which followed the publication in 1988 of *The Satanic Verses*. This novel, regarded by leaders and members of the Muslim community as blasphemous, led to the pronouncement of a death threat by the Ayatollah Khomeini against the author and to public burning of the book in Britain. These incidents resulted in an impassioned debate which gathered increasing momentum in the course of 1989 and 1990. To the Muslims their call for the banning of the book on grounds of blasphemy amounted to an assertion of what they regarded as their fundamental needs and aspirations. In other circles, however, the situation was viewed differently. To some critics of the Muslim stance the action of the anti-Rushdie forces amounted to an unwelcome assertion of communalist politics and an expression of fundamental contempt for the evolved values of British society. Indeed, to many people outside the Muslim fold the nature of the campaign against *The Satanic Verses* presented a striking example of Islamic intolerance.

Actions which affected Blacks and Asians in the form of discrimination in the labour market also need to be considered. In 1987 the Commission for Racial Equality (CRE), which had been established by the 1976 Race Relations Act, reported that Black and Asian applicants for chartered accountancy training were significantly less likely than their white contemporaries to receive offers of training contracts. Furthermore, a later CRE report revealed that Blacks and Asian minorities remained under-represented in the teaching profession and, more significantly, that teachers from these groups remained disproportionately represented on the lowest pay scale. Finally, a CRE enquiry published in January 1990 which examined the experiences of students graduating between 1982 and 1985 in securing first-time employment, found it difficult to resist the conclusion that racial discrimination influenced the greater difficulties experienced in this regard by Blacks and Asians.

One consequence of discrimination in the labour market manifested itself in the relatively high levels of unemployment which characterized Black and Asian groups in the 1980s. Evidence in support of the observation came in 1981 in a report on racial disadvantage by the Home Affairs Committee of the House of Commons which stressed that, 'At most times when it has been measured over the past ten years the rate of unemployment has been higher among ethnic minorities than among the rest of the population'.[9] The report regarded Blacks as particularly vulnerable and acknowledged that some, though not all, of this disadvantage related to discrimination. Later surveys, including the 1985 Labour Force Survey and the 1987 annual report of the Commission for Racial Equality, continued to draw attention to the persistence of relatively high levels of unemployment among Blacks and Asians.

Against this background, in the 1980s strong calls were heard from the CRE and similar organizations for positive action in order to assist the progress of such groups.

The advocacy of a policy initiative of this type amounted to a recognition that the opposition which Blacks and Asians faced in the labour market had become institutionalized. The term institutional racism is not without difficulties but, in drawing attention to the structural, rather than the personal, nature of the opposition which Blacks and Asians encountered, it serves an important function. The significance of such institutional forces has also been emphasized in discussions of Blacks and Asians and the housing market. In July 1987, for example, the press obtained details of an investigation by the CRE on the housing allocation policies of Tower Hamlets Council. The enquiry, which was officially published in the following year, concluded that the Council had engaged in discriminatory practices which particularly affected the Bangladeshi community. This action cannot be regarded as exceptional. In February 1989 the CRE issued a formal non-discrimination notice against Liverpool City Council after CRE officials had become convinced of the practice of racial discrimination in the city's housing department. Finally, the widespread reports of harassment and physical maltreatment of young Blacks and Asians by the police, particularly in inner-city areas, which occurred persistently in the course of the 1980s, together with reports of bullying within the Army, provided further signs of the extent of institutional pressures on these groups.

Violence against Blacks and Asians also occurred in other contexts throughout the 1980s. At the beginning of the decade a Home Office enquiry had confirmed the significance of the problem of racial attacks and the issue refused to go away in the course of the 1980s. A survey of press comment in May 1987 suggested its prevalence and another probing enquiry, drawing upon data collected in Leeds, Liverpool and Leicester, urged that 'the extent and seriousness of racial violence' needed to be fully recognized.[10] This hostility extended beyond the bleak streets of forbidding inner-city areas, even if it was often present there. By the 1980s racial attacks were occurring in schools: the murder of an Asian pupil at Burnage High School in Manchester in 1986 provided one tragic illustration of this trend. In the mid and late 1980s racial violence had also become a feature of prison life. Furthermore, although the public is generally aware of the degree of violence which surrounds association football – the attachment of some Fascist groups to Leeds United and Chelsea Football Clubs is often mentioned in this regard – by 1987 cricket had also been targeted by Fascist and racial nationalist groups as an area for carrying out racial attacks.

Faced with opposition and disadvantage and possessing only a limited representation in the power structure of British society – although that representation had increased since the major period of primary immigration in the 1950s and 1960s – one reaction of some Blacks and Asians in inner-city areas, along with other disadvantaged groups, came in the form of retaliation through violence. The Conservative Government's monetary experiment in the early years of the first Thatcher administration, designed as a shock treatment to revive British capitalism, cut deep economic scars into the inner-city areas, and Blacks in particular featured prominently in the mounting statistics on unemployment. This development, together with the heavy policing of inner-city districts, a policy consistent with the Government's commitment to law and order, generated continuing tension between minorities and police, with the latter becoming viewed as visible agents of institutional oppression. It was against this background that violence occurred. The urban unrest of the early 1980s is recalled by the general public primarily through the 'uprising' in Brixton and the ensuing Scarman Report, even though in that year violence flashed across the face of other areas, notably in Toxteth. Such events were followed in September–October 1985 by serious incidents in Handsworth, Brixton and particularly on the Broadwater Farm Estate in Tottenham. Against this cumulative background, the Director of the CRE warned in late 1987 of the prospect of future problems on a similar scale. If such violence achieved little by way of improvement for the inhabitants of the areas where it occurred, the events, particularly the violence in 1985, provided further ammunition for those sources hostile to the inner-city minorities. In concentrating on the manifestation rather than the causes of the violence such sources portrayed young Blacks in particular as a subversive element, an equivalent to the

nineteenth-century *classes dangereuses*, culturally alien, criminally
motivated in the sense of being consumed by a lust for loot, and
without any future in Britain. In other words, to a greater degree
than in 1980 and 1981, the events of 1985 were exploited in order to
question the belief in a multi-racial society. This shift of emphasis
has been viewed as yet another prominent indicator of the increasing racialization of British politics.

In recognizing the difficulties which Blacks and Asians have
faced in the recent past there would be a distortion in any account
which suggests that these groups have endured universal and
unremitting hostility in contemporary Britain. Oppression and
disadvantage did not possess a universal currency and its coin could
display complicated marks. In other words, in the 1980s, as in
earlier years, Blacks and Asians found supporters and defenders in
white society and discrimination often occurred in specific situations rather than as a general phenomenon. Furthermore, it is worth
reiterating that during these years individual Blacks and Asians had
forged successful careers. If individual success is not synonymous
with collective success, there is a need to recognize, nevertheless,
that in spite of discriminatory treatment which they faced, in the
1980s certain sections of the Asian population experienced low
levels of unemployment, lower, in fact, than those prevailing in the
white working population. Any attempt to overlook or obliterate
such complexities does a disservice to recent history.

The history of Ugandan Asians who arrived as refugees in 1972–3
is a case in point in arguing against a picture of all-pervading
gloom. The prospect of their immigration resulted in fierce expressions of opposition. The National Front mounted an early vigorous
campaign against their entry. Indeed, their arrival stimulated a
period of rapid growth for the Front which encouraged the formation in 1978 of its ideological opposite, the Anti-Nazi League.
Enoch Powell also marshalled popular forces of opposition against
the refugees. After other members of the Commonwealth agreed
to share in the task of resettlement, Edward Heath's administration
accepted that Britain did possess an obligation to these UK passport
holders: their status was similar to that of the Kenyan Asian refugees whose arrival in the late 1960s had also created fierce political
debate. This recognition led to the immigration of approximately

28,000 Ugandans. Nevertheless, the debate over their entry, like that of the Asians from Malawi soon afterwards, showed that restrictionist sentiment retained its vitality. It illustrated also that mounting and supporting an attack on an authoritarian government in Uganda – British public opinion lined up in strong opposition to Amin's regime – did not guarantee refugees from that country a tolerant welcome. As the *Sunday Telegraph* put it, 'A further swift influx of coloured immigrants to Britain is wholly undesirable on social grounds . . . The Uganda emergency must affect our ability to take any further immigration for the foreseeable future. If there are complaints, let them be addressed to President Amin and the blame put squarely at the door of black racialism'.[11]

Ten years later the perception of the Ugandan Asians had changed dramatically. By this time the Conservative press generally portrayed them in lavish terms as the personification of all those capitalist virtues which Britain's present Prime Minister had endowed with religious qualities. A study of this transition might take as its text, 'from vilification to apotheosis'.

This change is consistent with the concerted attempts of the Conservative Party from the late 1970s to attract Asian professional groups to its cause under the roof of organizations such as the Anglo-Asian Society. The 1983 Conservative election poster ('Labour says he's black, Tories say he's British')[12] indicated that, under certain conditions, some Blacks were also viewed as appropriate raw material for absorption into the Party. These initiatives have been used to argue that the Conservative commitment to free-market economics militates against the Party's acceptance of a full-blown racial nationalism.

In taking the post-war period as a whole, and aware of a number of positive developments and success stories, some commentators have argued that it is impossible to jettison all traces of optimism in considering the history of Blacks and Asians. This emphasis, to repeat, does deserve recognition. Nevertheless, the other side of the coin must be considered and the cumulative recent experiences of these groups cast a question mark over whether, without qualification, Britain can be viewed as a tolerant country.

By the 1980s immigration from the Commonwealth had been subjected to stringent controls. Such legislation and the rules associated with it, and the consequent restrictions on the development of minority populations, provided a clear indication of the death of the Commonwealth ideal which had still seemed strong at the end of the Second World War. In line with this changed perception it was not unknown for Black Commonwealth countries to be dismissed as 'assorted mango dictatorships'[13] and for the Commonwealth to be written off as a 'dud institution'.[14] Furthermore, throughout the 1980s neither Blacks and Asians who had secured entry, nor their British-born descendants could expect to escape totally from white hostility. Partly as a result of such pressures the majority of Blacks and Asians still remained locked into the socially disadvantaged groups. In addition, in view of the various continuing difficulties, including racial discrimination, whether overt or subtle, recognized or subconscious, which the children of these groups faced within the educational system, even if differences between groups in terms of attainment need to be recognized, no guarantee could be given that any substantial *general* upward social mobility would occur in the near future. Indeed, there is evidence to suggest that in the face of attacks on the so-called anti-racist policies pursued by various Local Education Authorities, these social engineering efforts underwent a retreat in the course of the late 1980s. The passions aroused by these policies during the so-called 'Honeyford affair' in Bradford which blew up between 1984 and 1986 marked only the tip of a wider volcanic issue.

Following on from this brief survey it might be asked what kind of picture emerges if a wider sweep of evidence, beginning in the late nineteenth century and concentrating particularly but not exclusively on immigrants and refugees, is considered.

II

A tolerant country?

Introduction

It is sometimes claimed that the history of Britain does not reveal any significant process of immigration. Policy makers keen to restrict recent entry have been quick to make this point: it was emphasized in 1956, for example, when Hungarian refugees began to arrive. In fact, the texture of British society is knitted together from many diverse strands and it would be difficult to unearth an epoch when the country did not have its share of immigrants and refugees and the minorities associated with such immigration.

Whereas there is a reluctance or inability to grasp the continuity of immigration many observers and commentators have been strikingly clear on a related issue, that those immigrants and refugees who did enter Britain were tolerated by members of the receiving society. This tolerant image has been internalized by many people. An awareness of this belief has already been noticed but it deserves more emphasis. In building up evidence on the strength of this public belief a comment by Herbert Butterfield made towards the end of the Second World War comes to mind: 'We teach and write the kind of history which is appropriate to our organization, to the intellectual climate of our part of the world'.[1] Written in the heat of international conflict it is a revealing observation and there is no doubt that considerable effort has been devoted to a portrayal of Britain as a country wedded to the virtues of liberty and toleration. A writer whose career and outlook contrasted sharply with Herbert Butterfield's nevertheless projected a vision of English society in which such values lay uppermost. In *The Lion and the Unicorn* George Orwell acknowledged the 'insularity' and 'xenophobia' of the English. However, he laid greater emphasis upon 'the gentleness of the English civilization' which constituted 'perhaps its marked characteristic'. After all, in this country 'bus conductors [were] good tempered and policemen [carried] no revolvers': society was characterized by a 'hatred of war and militarism' that was 'rooted deep in history'.[2] Here the essential liberties prevailed. What possible fears could be induced among immigrants and refugees and minorities in this comforting ambience?

On other occasions an emphasis on toleration appeared more directly. One such example came when, in its discussion of Fenian bombings in the nineteenth century, *The Times* dwelt on the strand of 'natural tolerance' in England which the Irish stood accused of abusing.[3] This direct emphasis on Britain as a fundamentally tolerant country is not restricted to nineteenth-century comment. After observing the differing experiences of Britain and a number of other European countries in relation to Fascism, one widely-used survey exploited that difference to dwell on the virtues of British 'decency'.[4] Furthermore, during the same years that Fascism emerged south of the border, militant Protestantism grew strongly in Scotland and a remark in *The Scotsman* at this time, expressing its hope that the 'reputation for culture and tolerance'[5] among the Scots would keep the arch-Protestants in check, revealed that a belief in toleration amounted to more than an exclusively English trait.

This clear emphasis on a tradition of toleration has been invoked particularly by the white British in discussions relating to the recent immigration from the Caribbean and the Indian sub-continent. In the autumn of 1958, following the collective violence which occurred in the summer of that year in Nottingham and Notting Hill, one Conservative MP drew attention to the 'ugly, frightening, primitive emotions' which had been put on display in Nottingham and London. At the same time he viewed this behaviour as an unfortunate aberration in a country which had 'hitherto always been regarded as the very cradle of liberty and tolerance, the most law-abiding country in the world'.[6] This same emphasis emerged at a later date when an observer of race relations in Britain remarked that 'the British people take a pride in their national tradition of freedom and justice'[7] and claimed that such qualities would work to the benefit of Black and Asian immigrants. In the 1960s similar sentiment can be found closer to the centre of British politics: a leading backbencher opposed any attempt to introduce a bill to outlaw racial discrimination in the confident expectation that this matter was best left to the 'tolerance and common sense'[8] which abounded in British society. The same virtuous note was struck in the 1965 White Paper on immigration in the claim that 'the good sense of the British people'[9] would help to minimize any friction over immigration. In short, all works for the best, a view thumped home in a recent newspaper editorial, 'we are a sovereign country, also a rather decent, humane country which owes nobody an apology for the treatment of black or brown people. Orwellian decency runs very deep in the British'.[10]

One of the heavy burdens constantly lying on the historian is to separate fact from fantasy. Just as Cromwell told the artist to paint him 'warts and all', there is a requirement on the historian to face evidence full square. There is a need to ascertain whether this widespread view of Britain as a tolerant country can withstand rigorous scrutiny. In considering this question it is impossible to cover all immigrant, refugee, and minority groups but a comprehensive cross-section of experiences can be brought into view.

Prologue 1871–1914

Can the Irish be regarded as an immigrant group? The 1801 Act of Union brought Ireland into union with England, Scotland and Wales and this constitutional arrangement stayed intact until the partition of Ireland in 1922. It might be argued that until such division the Irish should be treated as internal migrants. This distinction is not without interest, but general custom and practice ensure that even before the partition the Irish were classified as immigrants, and this categorization is freely adopted by Irish historians. If the Irish are classified as immigrants, there is no doubt that in the 'crown of thorns period', in the 1840s to the 1860s, they were widely perceived as constituting an economic and social problem. The image of Irish workers as a source of cheap labour and the general picture of them as polluters of urban life, are two powerful images which both reflected and influenced public responses during these difficult years.

However, did such antipathy linger into the late nineteenth century when the Irish-born (who numbered 774,310 in 1871 and 550,040 in 1911, with substantial settlements in Lancashire, London and the Glasgow area) constituted the largest single immigrant group in Britain? On one hand, any discussion needs to be tentative, since large tracts of their history during these years remain unrecovered, though the areas which have been exposed to view tend to reveal an encouraging picture. One can understand why: by the late nineteenth century the Irish and men of Irish descent can be found in positions of prominence in the trade union movement. The inference is that these people were being assimilated into the working class in Britain and its associated structures. Signs of individual success by some of the better-off Irish have also been given prominence. This evidence cannot be ignored, but neither can the more obscure and less favourable parts of the overall picture.

Over many years the Irish had been portrayed as savages under British domination. This cultural conditioning did not disappear overnight: once formed, stereotypes tend to display massive resilience. Consequently when they arrived in Britain the Irish continued to suffer from this labelling, which sometimes assumed a racial dimension. Furthermore, Irish Catholics had to face the heat of religious opposition. Indeed, one commentator suggested that anti-Catholic sentiment possessed a stronger force in Liverpool than in any other city in the United Kingdom with the exception of Belfast. On occasions such religious antipathy became converted into sectarian violence. Also, in Scotland, within the trade union movement, old tensions of Protestant versus Catholic, which translated easily into Scots versus Irish, had not disappeared. Finally, developments associated with Irish nationalism also spilled over to affect the lives of the Irish across the water. One dramatic illustration of it came in 1882 with the nationwide attacks on the Irish minority following the murder in Phoenix Park of Lord Frederick Cavendish and Thomas Burke. When these details are added to the continuing suspicion of the Irish as a source of cheap labour, a more varied picture than that which treats Erin's exiles as an increasingly tolerated group begins to emerge, even though hostility varied between regions (on Tyneside and in Dundee, owing to local conditions, it remained relatively weak) and the opposition generally might have lacked the sharp, cutting edge of the mid-nineteenth century years.

The accumulated immigrant groups from continental Europe remained dwarfed in size by the Irish but their presence raised a number of important issues. One European group which did increase in the late nineteenth century was the Italian-born population. It numbered 5,331 in 1871 and and 24,983 in 1911. As in the case of the Irish some division in public responses can be identified. The affluent middle class who welcomed the services of Italian waiters did not hare the British waiters' fear of competition. However, on other issues, such as the exploitation of children by Italian musicians, a common front of antipathy might be revealed.

In turning attention towards continental European groups it is necessary to consider others besides the Italians. Until the 1891 census the Germans constituted the largest population from continental Europe. In 1871 a total of 32,833 Germans appeared in the census, and by 1911 the group had increased to 53,324. These Germans constituted a heterogeneous group, embracing clerks, waiters, governesses and, higher up the social scale, bankers, financiers and industrialists, as well as, briefly, a handful of German gypsies.

Virtually every strand of the community encountered hostility at some point. German clerks, welcomed by commercial houses in the City of London and business concerns in provincial centres such as Manchester, ran into hostility from English clerks. The whiff of opposition comes strongly off the pages of the *Clerks' Journal* in the 1880s. Some of the sharpest antipathy, however, was reserved for the German gypsies who began to arrive in 1904. By the later nineteenth century the established gypsy population in Britain was under continued attack from various quarters. Missionaries thirsted to convert the heathen, and through the provisions of the Moveable Dwellings Bills politicians attempted to circumscribe the travellers' freedom. Voices raised in support of the gypsies made little impression. It is against this background, and the fierce debate over alien immigration triggered off by the arrival of newcomers from Russian Poland, that the history of the German gypsies must be considered. Their stay proved to be short-lived. 'How are we to get rid of these wretched people?'[11] asked Sir Howard Vincent, Tory MP for Sheffield Central, in the House of Commons. He did not have to wait long for an answer. Between 1905 and 1906 the few hundred German gypsies were despatched, with the connivance and support of the state, to Europe where a generation later they would almost certainly have ended up in one of Hitler's camps. This small, weak, indeed powerless group, experienced nothing of the fabled toleration of the British.

What, however, of the rich Germans, many of whom were Jews? This section of the community included men such as Ernest Cassel, the financier, and Felix Semon, the surgeon, both of whom had become prominent in Britain early in the present century. Such social standing implied that, for these Germans, Britain amounted to an open, tolerant society in which they, and contemporaries of similar status, could function without hindrance. It is certainly true that Jews did not find any formal anti-Jewish hurdles. By the late nineteenth century Jews had been emancipated and were free in law to pursue careers open to their talents.

In the case of the so-called 'Court Jews', close to the monarchy, the high point of their fortunes came in the reign of Edward VII and his death coincided with a change in their status. Max Beerbohm's cartoon, *Are we as welcome as ever?*[12] caught the new uncertain ambience. However, the death of the King amounted to only one factor which affected their fortunes. Following the defeat of France in the Franco-Prussian War of 1870–1, a fear of German militarism developed. George Chesney's *The Battle of Dorking* (1870–1) speculated on the prospects of a German invasion of Britain and a strain of anti-Germanism continued to seep into a phalanx of popular literature. This fear of a future war with Germany increased in the early twentieth century. At the same time tension developed over the increasing commercial rivalry between the two countries. In these circumstances, when military and commercial fears interacted, spy fever flourished and to Leo Maxse, the editor of the *National Review*, virtually every activity by Germans in the years immediately preceding the Great War was undertaken in the interests of their mother country. In presenting the message Maxse did not hesitate to stir in a lavish ladle of anti-semitism. The lesson is that toleration of the Germans was conditional: in the early twentieth century Germany became increasingly regarded as a major threat to Britain and this international rivalry had a negative impact on the German immigrant community, particularly on its rich and powerful members. The admiration of German efficiency and the sense of cultural affinity between Britain and Germany, both of which had been emphasized in earlier years, became replaced by a sense of social paranoia and a growing antipathy towards Germans.

In the late nineteenth century the Jewish community had been supplemented not only by Jews from Germany but also by a growing number of immigrants from Russian Poland. By 1911 the Russian Polish population in England and Wales numbered 95,541 and in Scotland also the Russian Poles constituted the largest continental European group. A large number of these Russian Poles were Jewish although the census returns did not identify them as such.

It has been noted that before these immigrants arrived the Jewish population had been emancipated. Legislation which entered the statute-book between 1826 and 1871 freed the minority from its former disabilities. By the late nineteenth century Britain had witnessed the entry of Jews into both Houses of Parliament and Disraeli, born a Jew but a convert to Christianity, had been Prime Minister. Taken together with evidence on religious, commercial and professional freedom, a first impression might be that in Britain a tolerant compact had been secured with the Jews whose apex of achievement and power resided in the so-called 'Cousinhood' of important, influential families.

However, anti-semitism had not withered away. Hostile images and stereotypes created over the centuries did not suddenly disappear in the age of liberal emancipation. On the contrary, in specific circumstances these images helped to direct hostility not only towards the Russian Poles and the German Jews but also onto the longer-established community.

Some voices spoke out in defence of the Russian Poles but these were drowned by the greater choir of opposition. Competition in the housing and labour markets resulted in some of the sharpest conflict. In areas of settlement such as the East End of London, Leeds and Manchester a cultural antipathy also developed against the inclination of the newcomers to live 'according to their traditions, usages and customs'.[13] In addition, fears developed that there might be 'grafted onto the English stock . . . the debilitated sickly and vicious products of Europe'.[14] This species of opposition leaped from the pages of Joseph Banister's *England under the Jews* which first appeared in 1901. These spoken and written forms of opposition were supplemented by action in the sense that Jews encountered discrimination. Furthermore, for several years after 1901 a mobilization of opposition against the Russian Poles can be detected in the activities of the British Brothers' League. Finally, incidents such as the attacks on Jews in Tredegar in August 1911 constitute a reminder that the Russian Poles did not manage to avoid the terror of collective violence. These issues relating to Jewish immigration added a cutting edge to the general debate on alien immigration in the late nineteenth and early twentieth centuries.

The Jewish élite also encountered problems during these years. One recurring theme related to the question of Jewish loyalty. Were Jews intent on pursuing sectional interests? Did they perceive themselves as a committed, integral part of British society? The emancipation contract could not douse this smouldering, long-standing issue which burst into life at the time of the Eastern Crisis in the 1870s, during the South African War of 1899–1902, as well as in the course of the Marconi scandal of 1911 and the Indian Silver scandal of the same year. Combined with other evidence such as that drawn from literature and the music hall, and bearing in mind a number of well-publicized cases of discrimination, it becomes clear that anti-semitism remained a persistent feature of liberal Britain before the First World War.

Apart from European groups, the population mosaic of British society before the First World War contained an Afro-Caribbean population and various sub-continental Asian groups. A small Chinese community can also be found. This last group remained miniscule. The 1911 census recorded only 1,319 Chinese aliens, although the figure was swollen to an uncertain but nevertheless minor extent by those Chinese who originated in dependencies of the British crown. However, its paltry size did not shield this group from hostility. Since it is often assumed that a small immigrant, refugee, or minority group can avoid opposition it is worth exploring why this failed to occur in the case of the Chinese. Images drawn from reports of missionaries and travellers provided a framework within which this group could be viewed and two strands from these perceptions, the diligence of the Chinese and their moral backwardness, were seized upon in specific situations and turned against them. What shipowners regarded as the diligence of Chinese seamen could smack to merchant seamen of cheap docile labour. This conflict over employment, which led to major campaigns being mounted against the Chinese by the National Sailors' and Firemen's Union (NSFU), provided the immediate background to the attacks on Chinese property in Cardiff in 1911. However, the widespread nature of this violence suggests deeper tensions were present. In attempting an explanation it is necessary to count the allegations of sexual irregularities which a male-dominated Chinese group had to face and their alleged association with other morally corrupting activities such as gambling and opium smoking. Sometimes a *mélange* of such claims compounded the weight of opposition. Perceptions were also influenced by the wider context of the 'Yellow Peril', the threat from the East. It is no accident that Sax Rohmer's first Fu Manchu novel appeared in 1913. It is against this cumulative negative picture that individual expressions of support such as that from an East End woman identified in one popular survey can be set. She had married a Chinese as a second husband and much preferred him to the Irish man with whom she had first settled down. Whether or not she had a general sympathy for the Chinese remains unknown.

In considering the years between 1871 and 1914 a start has been made on questioning the commonly heard emphasis on Britain as a tolerant country. These years provide abundant evidence of written and spoken hostility as well as discrimination and collective violence. Moreover, in 1905, through the Aliens Act, which resulted from the debate surrounding Russian Polish immigration, a decisive breach occurred in the policy which since 1826 had allowed the unrestricted entry of aliens into Britain. The 1905 Aliens Act, one of the measures by which the Conservative Government hoped to drive a wedge between Liberals and Labour by demonstrating the Unionist Party's solidarity with Labour, laid down that immigrant ships, defined as those vessels carrying twenty or more steerage passengers, were required to berth at designated ports. Immigration officers at these ports of disembarkation could refuse entry to such passengers (in effect those who did not travel first or second class) for a variety of reasons. If, in the opinion of the officer, an immigrant lacked the means of support or seemed incapable of acquiring such means, sufficient grounds existed for exclusion. Lunacy, disease, a sentence abroad for an extraditable offence (except for political crimes), and the existence of an expulsion order made previously under the 1905 Act, constituted other grounds for refusing entry. The open door had closed: entry for aliens became a discretionary rather than an absolute right. In addition, certain categories of aliens could be expelled from the country. Legislators had the criminal alien in mind here. But in all, a long tradition had been broken. Nevertheless, this legislation did not end the public debate on immigration from Russian Poland and it did nothing to quell the suspicions surrounding the German-born population in Britain. On the contrary, this group became increasingly exposed as Europe drifted towards war and it faced even stronger opposition once hostilities began.

The First World War and its aftermath

The outbreak of war tends both to divide and to reinforce. The overwhelming tendency is to draw a distinction between 'them' and 'us'. As a result it comes as no surprise that the Germans, now classified as enemy aliens, faced opposition. An exclusive concentration on this antipathy, however, would miss strands of hostility encountered by friendly aliens. The opposition directed towards these groups, the Belgians and the Russian Poles, is particularly significant in revealing the limits of toleration in Britain.

With the outbreak of war in August 1914, the German-born

group stood starkly exposed to hostility. Any remaining admiration for Germany and Germans vanished, to be supplanted by fear and loathing. Whereas the 1905 Aliens Act had been agonized over, in August 1914 a stricter Aliens Act, which placed controls over the registration, movement and deportation of all aliens, passed through the House in a single day. There can be no doubt that, whatever general controls were introduced, the German-born featured prominently in the minds of those who legislated. A clear indication that stern action by the authorities could draw upon strong public support came with the violence directed in that same August against the Germans in centres such as London and Keighley.

In 1915 a significant intensification of anti-German sentiment became noticeable, particularly after the sinking, off the coast of Ireland in May 1915, of the passenger liner, the *Lusitania*. 'I call for a Vendetta', Horatio Bottomley wrote in *John Bull*, 'a vendetta against every German in Britain whether "naturalised" or not . . . you cannot naturalise an unnatural beast – a human abortion – a hellish freak. But you *can* exterminate it. And now the time has come'.[15] D. H. Lawrence, moved by a spasm of violent anti-German outrage, wrote to Lady Ottoline Morrell: 'I am mad with rage myself. I would like to kill a million Germans – two million'.[16]

This popular anti-Germanism, supplemented at times by doses of anti-semitism, surged up at particular stages of the war. Apart from 1914 and 1915 it assumed considerable strength in 1918 at the time of the German offensive on the Western Front. It also embraced more than manic prose and vicious sentiment. In 1915, after considerable social pressure, a number of prominent public figures, including Ernest Cassel and Felix Semon, signed loyalty letters in *The Times*. Some important German-born figures such as Prince Louis of Battenberg were drummed out of public life, and Lord Haldane, widely regarded as sympathetic to German culture, was dismissed from the Cabinet. The weight of official action manifested itself most dramatically in the policy of internment. As a result of this initiative the Government set up internment camps across the country into which enemy alien men were herded by the British authorities. It has been estimated that the government incarcerated 32,000 men in the camps of whom 24,500 remained there at the end of the war. With a greater degree of reluctance, based essentially on expedient considerations, the Government also engaged in the repatriation of enemy aliens. In this particular exercise, carried out between 1914 and 1919, it has been calculated that the authorities removed 28,774 enemy aliens from Britain, of whom 23,571 had German origins.

In all these developments there can be traced the interaction of popular and official sentiment. Government propaganda on alleged atrocities by the German Army in Belgium, for example, fed into popular anti-Germanism, which in turn assisted the evolution of official policy. It had been consequent upon the German invasion of Belgium that Britain entered the war and events in that country not only helped to fuel anti-German sentiment but also resulted in the arrival of Belgian refugees in Britain.

As might be expected, the Belgians initially received considerable public sympathy. They were singled out by private philanthropic organizations which did all they could to assist the refugees, although the scale of the problem became so great – more than 200,000 Belgians arrived between 1914 and 1918 – that eventually the state assumed responsibility for the exiles. Nevertheless, the fund of public sympathy did not extend into all sectors of British society. *The Times* commented adversely on the 'cataract'[17] of Belgians and portrayed them as engaged in an invasion. Some opposition also came from within the trade union movement which remained keen to protect the interests of British workers.

Friendly aliens from Belgium were not the only allies who encountered opposition in war-time Britain. The Russian Poles had to contend with various strands of antipathy. Some accusations turned upon their alleged involvement in war-time profiteering. A deeper source of tension, however, which assumed anti-semitic dimensions, developed after the introduction in 1916 of military conscription. The men who entered the field against Germany in the First World War were volunteers or regular soldiers. With the dashing of any hopes that the war might be over by Christmas 1914 and particularly with the growing slaughter at the front, this early wild enthusiasm for the war evaporated and it became progressively difficult to find men to sign up and take the King's shilling. In 1916, as a consequence, the British Government decided to introduce conscription. In these circumstances an accelerating antipathy became directed towards the Russian Polish community.

Anglo-Jewry played a full active part in the war: the black-edged death rolls in the *Jewish Chronicle* constitute a sombre reminder of this sacrifice. However, in areas such as Leeds and the East End of London, tensions developed over the avoidance of military service by Russian Poles. Any inclination in Government circles to avoid this sensitive issue had to reckon with the strength of local feeling against these Jews, which was assiduously and secretly conveyed to the Government in police reports. In their defence the Russian Poles raised a number of objections against military service. Why should they fight for a Tsar who had persecuted them?, some men asked. Socialists in the ghetto expressed their objection to any involvement in a capitalists' war. In these circumstances, when the voluntary recruiting campaign failed, the British Government passed the Military Service (Allied Conventions) Act in August 1917. As a result, with the approval of the Tsarist authorities, Russian Poles of military age received the option of serving in either the British or the Russian Army. This arrangement came too late to avoid a major outbreak of violence in Leeds in June 1917 and could not prevent serious hostility in Bethnal Green in September 1917. Both incidents arose over the conscription issue and provide another reminder that at times hostility towards immigrants became translated into collective violence.

Further evidence of antipathy being converted into action came in 1919 with the passing in that year of the Aliens Act, which, with subsequent Orders in Council, remained in force until 1971. In the debate leading up to the Act vicious expressions of anti-alienism abounded. 'We do not want German blood any more in this country', one Member told the House, 'We have had it in high places and we want no more'.[18] Other groups such as the Russian Poles encountered similar vituperation. The most powerful strand of sentiment running through the debate was summarized by Horatio Bottomley, now elevated from the editor's chair at *John Bull* to a seat in the Commons: 'Britain for the British, socially and industrially',[19] constituted the theme of his hostile intervention.

The 1919 Act endowed the State through the agency of the Home Secretary and immigration officers with considerable powers over the entry, employment and deportation of aliens. Entry was restricted to a number of approved ports and became conditional upon the possession of a work permit. Once admitted, all aliens had to register locally with the police. Expulsion could be enforced if an alien engaged in attempts to foment sedition or disaffection. Those of less than two years' residence who ventured to cause industrial unrest could also be deported. There is no doubt that the Act constituted an important landmark in the State's control over alien immigration. 'The liberal procedures of the Victorian age and indeed of the years between 1905 and 1914 belonged to a different and vanished world.'[20]

The deportation of Russian Polish Jews was already taking place under existing legislation as the 1919 Bill passed through Parliament and the state continued with the removal of those Jewish aliens who fell foul of the 1919 Act. In the immediate post-war years official policy towards aliens also created problems for the Lithuanian minority from the Russian Empire. After the 1917 Military Service Act many Lithuanians had opted for a return to Russia and enlistment in the Tsar's army. This move amounted to a calculated gamble based on the assumption that the whole operation would be bungled by the British and Russian authorities, with the result that military service would be avoided. The gamble, always a long shot, failed. For some Lithuanians it turned particularly sour when the British Government refused to re-admit those who were unable to provide evidence of military service in the allied cause during the war or during the allied intervention campaigns after the Bolshevik Revolution. Proof was elusive, as the Government knew quite well. As a result, Lithuanian families became separated. Women and children torn away from their menfolk received Treasury support until the end of 1920. Then, however, the withdrawal of Government funds forced these families to accept the British Government's 'offer' of repatriation. Between February and March 1920 the authorities repatriated six hundred Lithuanian women and children in this exercise.

The 1919 Aliens Act entered the statute-book in the atmosphere of uncertainty which prevailed during the transition from war to peace. In this context, and in the same year, outbreaks of collective violence occurred across Britain. The violence in Liverpool and

South Wales, particularly in Cardiff, directed against a range of so-called 'coloured' groups, has captured most attention. However, similar incidents broke out in a number of other centres, including Salford, Hull and Glasgow and in some cases persisted into the 1920s.

It has been claimed that these events need to be set against the images and expectations which had resulted from the exploitation of imperial groups. But immediate pressures also loomed large in the picture. Competition for employment, particularly in an over-stocked labour market in the shipping industry and a general white resentment at the gains achieved during the war by the 'coloured' population, as it was categorized in a hazy, slapdash fashion, helped to generate the violence that summer. For its part the Government loaded responsibility for the events of 1919 onto Black British subjects and attempted to secure their repatriation.

There can be no doubt that the history of immigrants, refugees and minorities in Britain during the period of the First World War and its immediate aftermath is tinged with violence. It comes as no surprise, however, that these developments have received relatively little attention. Incidents such as the 'anti-black reign of terror'[21] which gripped Liverpool in the summer of 1919 sound a jarring note to those who believe passionately in the celebrated toleration of British society: they are hardly able to contemplate attacks on enemy aliens, let alone on allies or British subjects.

The inter-war years 1919–1939

The economic dislocation of the inter-war years placed a brake upon the process of international migration. At the same time, these economic changes helped to produce new political structures, and in turn the emergence of Fascism generated a flow of refugees within Europe and also beyond its boundaries. Some of these left Italy and Spain for new lives elsewhere but the major focus of international interest has been directed towards the exiles from the Greater Germany. The reception of these refugees needs to be considered. Before that, however, the Irish can be brought once more into the picture.

On the eve of the First World War the Irish had been the largest single immigrant group in Britain. In the 1931 census this position was maintained even though they amounted to only 1 per cent of the total population. An examination of the still fragmentary history of the Irish during the inter-war years suggests that many echoes of earlier forms of hostility continued to sound. The 'No Irish'[22] signs in the Midlands revealed that employment did not always come easily. The deep well of sectarian differences also continued to be drawn upon for political advantage. In the 1931 general election H. D. Longbottom, the candidate for Protestant Democracy in one of the Liverpool constituencies, held immigration from Ireland and the presence of a minority of Irish descent to be responsible for the problem of unemployment in Liverpool as well as for the continued existence of slums and the city's high rates. Such opposition directed towards the Catholic Irish smacked of the same hostility that identified Jews as responsible for all the social problems of the inter-war East End of London; it also presaged some of the opposition directed at a later date towards Black and Asian minorities.

Political developments in other parts of Britain also affected the reception of the Irish. Scottish nationalism received a powerful boost from the economic and social problems which Scotland faced during the inter-war years and within the nationalist camp a clear strand of hostility emerged towards the Southern Irish, though it did not achieve a universal sway. Irish Catholics in Scotland also fell foul of militant Protestant organizations such as Alexander Ratcliffe's Scottish Protestant League (launched in 1920) and John Cormack's Protestant Action Society (founded in 1933), within both of which a fierce anti-Irish Catholic sentiment burned. These groups were firmly located on the extreme fringe of Protestantism but a report called *The Menace of the Irish Race to our Scottish Nationality*, submitted in 1923 to the general assembly of the Church of Scotland, indicated that at times anti-Irish, anti-Catholic sentiment moved closer towards the centre of Scottish social and religious life.

Developments in the history of Irish nationalism also continued to touch the lives of the Irish and those of Irish descent. The execution in Dublin, on 21 November 1920, of a number of British Army officers and auxiliary policemen led to attacks on certain

'Irish' pubs in London. At a later date the 1939 offensive by the IRA (Irish Republican Army), culminating in a bomb attack in Coventry, immediately soured attitudes towards the Irish and their descendants in the Midlands where, in the inter-war years, some had found work in the car industry and engineering trades. The bombing campaign also resulted in inter-communal tensions in Liverpool and Glasgow and the beating-up of an IRA prisoner in Dartmoor. Memories did not quickly fade and the remembrance of the bombing continued to stimulate anti-Irish hostility long after the immediate sound of the bombs had died away.

Campaigns by the IRA have often resulted in the Irish being portrayed as animals, particularly as apes. Such imagery derived from a longer tradition which racialized the Irish, and during the inter-war years it is possible to detect a continuation of such racial stereotyping. In Liverpool, for example, the opposition of G. R. Gair, the anthropologist, which was based on biological and related cultural grounds, assumed a clear racist dimension, and some of the hostility from Scottish nationalists possessed a similar tone.

In spite of such varied opposition, the British placed no restrictions on immigration from the Irish Free State. The partition of Ireland in 1922 did not result in the erection of any barriers to citizens of that country. In that respect they fared better than any group of European aliens. Even so, proposals to control immigration from Southern Ireland did come before the British Parliament in 1929, 1932, 1934–35 and 1937. If no legislation entered the statute-book, optimistic commentators on the Irish in Britain still need to ponder on the pressures which placed the prospect of entry controls on the political agenda at Westminster.

In comparison with the Irish considerable attention has been lavished on refugees who arrived in Britain from the Greater Germany. It might be supposed that these groups huddling in exile from Nazism would be accorded a tolerant welcome, even if they were not totally accepted.

Some individuals and groups in Britain did adopt a pro-refugee position. However, in general, responses were less favourable. Professional groups among the refugees had to face opposition from their British contemporaries. This issue reached a climax with the admission of refugees from Austria following the enforced union of Austria and Germany in 1938. The British Medical Association managed to secure an agreement with the Home Office to control the arrival of refugee doctors and their subsequent employment in Britain. Architects and academics added to the anxious professional voices who spoke out against the refugees, but it was not only professional groups who encountered opposition: child refugees and domestics also met with antipathy. Against that background Fascist groups played the refugee card and if in Parliament the refugees found a consoling voice in Josiah Wedgwood and a smattering of support among other members, hostile expressions also surfaced. Captain A. H. M. Ramsay, the Tory MP for Peebles and a Fascist sympathizer, was the most prominent among these but other members made a contribution to the hostility.

Those at the centre of British politics showed no great enthusiasm for the arrival of the refugees. The substantial powers vested in the Home Secretary by the 1919 Aliens Act were used restrictively by all Governments throughout the inter-war years. This alone guaranteed a cautious approach towards the arrival of refugees from central Europe. Until 1938 the right to enter Britain was granted predominantly to those refugees who had the prospect of moving eventually to another country. Some easing of controls over entry occurred in the autumn of 1938 and continued into 1939, partly as a result of the lobbying of pro-refugee groups. The criticism which descended on the system of harsh entry controls into Palestine, where Britain had exercised the mandate for the League of Nations since 1922, also led the Government to grant concessions over entry to Britain and the Empire, by way of compensation. In the event, some 56,000 refugees arrived in Britain from central Europe in the course of the 1930s and one assessment of official policy has described it as 'comparatively compassionate, even generous'.[23] However, in view of the harsh restrictive policies pursued in other countries this positive assessment should not be over-emphasized.

How is it possible to account for the opposition which the refugees encountered? They came to a country seriously afflicted by the crisis in the world economy and by all the anxiety and hardship this collapse created. In these circumstances fears in the labour market can be understood. However, a wider perspective is required. The anti-Germanism which surrounded the debate on the 1919 Aliens Act still lingered. So did the anti-semitism which entered into those discussions. Many of the exiles from central Europe were Jewish and although Jewish agencies offered to prevent such refugees becoming a burden on the public funds, in official circles a fear persisted that a generous entry policy would aid the development of anti-semitism. No doubt part of this fear involved a projection of the anti-Jewish sentiments of those politicians and civil servants involved in the formulation of policy. It also reflected an awareness of the tradition of anti-semitism in Britain which baulked at the prospect of an increasing number of Jewish exiles. In other words, in the Hitler age, the Government remained conscious of public opposition towards Jews. Official policies capitulated to this sentiment and simultaneously reflected and reinforced it.

Where is the evidence for the claim that a general anti-semitism can be identified in inter-war Britain? In the 1920s, a powerful boost was given to such antipathy by the 1917 Bolshevik Revolution, with which Jews became widely identified. The relationship of Jews to Bolshevism was complex but in politics simple connections are often sought and in some circles the Revolution became portrayed as the first giant step in a Jewish world conspiracy. A fear of Jewish domination had been present in Britain before 1917 and, given sustenance by the Revolution, by 1920 it seemed in some quarters that the message of *The Protocols of the Elders of Zion* was coming to fruition. Notwithstanding Philip Graves's exposé of *The Protocols* which appeared in *The Times* in the summer of 1921 (an English translation of the work had appeared in Britain in 1920), a belief in a Jewish world conspiracy persisted tenaciously throughout the 1920s and even later particularly in racial nationalist circles and among certain High Tory groups.

Conspiratorial theories aside, other evidence of anti-semitic thought can be culled from the 1920s. To cite one example, Karl Pearson, the biometrician, still dwelt on the immigration from Russian Poland and argued a case for the exclusion of such Jews on biological grounds. These instances of conspiratorial theory and scientific–racist anti-semitism added to the persistent amorphous anti-Jewish sentiment which circulated in Britain. The history of the Jewish community was also influenced by the continuation of social discrimination and certain official policies at both national and local level. The problems faced by Jewish aliens consequent upon the 1919 Aliens Act have already been observed. During the 1920s alien Jews also had to contend with the discrimination practised by the London County Council authority in its employment, housing and educational policies.

It is the 1930s, however, rather than the 1920s which reveal the apogee of anti-semitism in inter-war Britain. Several developments endow these years with particular significance. Fascist groups had been established in the 1920s but their political heyday arrived in the 1930s in the wake of the international economic crisis. The Imperial Fascist League, an organization which is usually, indeed excessively, linked with A.S. Leese, placed an antipathy towards Jews at the centre of its political programme. However, any account of Fascism in the 1930s brings even more to mind the activities of Oswald Mosley and the British Union of Fascists. In his autobiography, *My Life,* published in 1968, in which he collected his political reflections in tranquility, Mosley firmly denied that he had ever been an anti-semite. He claimed that he attacked Jews for what they did rather than for what they were. This defence, which sounded the first shot in a continuing campaign to 'rehabilitate' Mosley, is unconvincing. Mosley did betray traces of anti-semitism, particularly when his rational mask slipped, and there can be no doubt that anti-semitism pullulated within his organization, particularly after 1934, although it can be detected from the movement's early days.

Fascist anti-semitism is relatively easy to detect, but Fascism did not possess a monopoly of anti-semitic sentiment in the 1930s. It appeared in High-Tory circles on the pages of the *Patriot* and *Truth.* It continued to flourish within the Chesterbelloc circle which had never forgotten the Marconi scandal. G. K. Chesterton and Hilaire Belloc were both prominent Catholics, and Catholic anti-semitism, over which a veil is often discreetly drawn, continued to be a source of anxiety to Anglo-Jewry in the inter-war years. In addition, it is necessary to look beyond these parameters and recognize the continuing wide diffusion of an amorphous anti-semitism in Britain in the 1930s. Popular novels of these years and private comment in diaries reveal the persistence and extent of such sentiment.

Jews also continued to encounter discrimination throughout the 1930s. The *Jewish Chronicle* assiduously reported on advertisements such as that in the *Daily Telegraph* which, advertising a typing vacancy, stipulated 'No Jewesses', and the announcement in the *Hackney Gazette* which offered unfurnished rooms but laid down that 'no children or Jews' would be accepted.[24] Some Jews found themselves on the receiving end of another form of action in the 1930s which came in the shape of collective violence. In the East End particularly, Jews had to contend with the fists and boots of Mosley's boys in black. Memories of that conflict stay vivid in the minds of those who experienced it.

Looking back on all this evidence we can but echo the observation of one perceptive observer of the time: 'Anti-semitism was in the air: an unmistakable tang'.[25] It is against this background, and bearing in mind that those at the centre of political life in Whitehall and Westminster breathed the same cultural air, that anti-semitism can be viewed as a general phenomenon and an influence over official policy in the inter-war years.

Before quitting these years, the histories of the Black minority and of other groups from the Empire need to be considered. The violence of 1919 and subsequent years, together with the economic problems of the inter-war period, contributed to a reduction in the level of immigration from the Empire between 1919 and 1939. Even so, some inward movement occurred. The gathering of intellectuals and students at the 'junction box' of the Empire, evident also in earlier years, provided one part of this picture. Jomo Kenyatta, George Padmore, and C. L. R. James can be counted among the Black newcomers, and activists such as Krishna Menon came from the Indian sub-continent. These individuals might have avoided the hostility in the labour market that their working-class contemporaries encountered, but they could hardly escape other rebuffs. The high hopes which many students carried with them on their long journeys to Britain often started to crumble on first contact, as they tried to find accommodation, for example. 'It isn't as if it was me, dearie, but I've got me other gentlemen to consider',[26] the landlady's rejection which continued to ring in the ears of Kwame Nkrumah, had been heard earlier by many Black students. Indeed, such discrimination, against which no legal redress existed, had been one of the pressures encouraging Ladipo Solanke to form the West African Students' Union (WASU) in 1925.

Students were sojourners, transients who came and went. So too were many of the political activists. During the inter-war years, however, a settled Black population lived in Britain and the experiences of this small group – its size cannot be estimated with any worthwhile degree of accuracy – make depressing reading. Surveys tended to portray the group as a social-pathological minority. Children of mixed race origins, the so-called 'half-castes', appeared as a particular problem. The sympathetic account of this group in Cedric Dover's *Half-Caste* was exceptional. The fact that some of these children had been born into stable relationships – in itself an indication that anti-Black hostility did not hold universal sway – made no substantial impression on those individuals and groups who dominated the investigative surveys of the inter-war years. Indeed, societies established to work on behalf of Blacks could sometimes share in the general hostility. One example of this tendency can be found in the Anti-Slavery Society which was originally set up after the First World War to administer the Welfare of Africans in Europe War Fund. A few years later the Society became 'the first real lobby specifically opposing black immigration' to appear in Britain.[27]

An exclusive concentration on the production of pamphlets and the activities of pressure groups misses other major developments which influenced the history of Blacks. During the inter-war years severe problems developed in the international shipping industry, particularly in the tramp shipping trade. In these circumstances, especially in ports such as Cardiff 'the most bitter economic competition between white and coloured seamen took place'.[28] As a result of pressure from the National Sailors' and Firemen's Union, the Special Restriction (Coloured Alien Seamen) Order was published in 1925. This Order closed a loophole in the 1919 Aliens Act which some alien seamen had been quick to exploit. The 1925 measure placed restrictions on the entry and employment of such workers, but in its enforcement it developed a wider significance. According to one commentator, 'whereas it had once been accepted that most of the coloured population in Cardiff were British subjects, now the onus of proof was placed upon the coloured man'.[29] In Cardiff the police applied the Order so rigorously that few seamen could establish their British identity. Those unable to furnish such evidence found themselves consigned to the dole queue. These problems intensified in 1936 following the introduction in the previous year of the British Shipping (Assistance) Act which allowed for the payment of subsidies to the tramp shipping business but stipulated that first preference in the recruitment of firemen and seamen should be given to workers of British nationality. Following this measure those British seamen in Cardiff, drawn from various parts of the Empire, who had been converted into aliens by the action of the local state, became further exposed and vulnerable. After a concerted campaign against such manifest injustice British citizenship was eventually restored to more than 1,600 men. Nevertheless, the sense of bitterness at their treatment was not easily washed away. Viewed in a sober historical perspective there are few clearer cases of the institutional oppression of minorities in early twentieth-century Britain.

The wartime years 1939–1945

In the First World War British society drew together in the face of a common foe, and in so doing identified its internal enemies. In such circumstances enemy aliens could expect little toleration. A similar development can be detected during the Second World War. Between 1914 and 1918 difficulties also arose with allied groups. This development was also mirrored between 1939 and 1945.

Those groups which became known as enemy aliens provide a convenient starting point. With certain exceptions, visas granted before the war to enemy nationals ceased to be valid from 11.00 a.m. on 3 September 1939, the day that Britain declared war on Germany, two days after the German invasion of Poland. Jewish refugees who attempted to enter Palestine discovered that entry into the mandated territory also remained tightly controlled. Throughout the war, in fact, Britain pursued a strict immigration policy in Britain, the Empire, and Palestine.

Those refugees who had already managed to enter Britain soon realized that no restful bed was available on which they could recuperate from their previous traumas. The war-time history of Jewish refugees underlines this claim. Even though the Allies fought a war against Germany, a country where anti-semitism had become a salient feature of public policy, anti-semitism did not suddenly disappear from Britain. It persisted throughout the war to affect the lives of Jewish refugees, and extended to those Jews who had been born in Britain.

The dismissal of Leslie Hore-Belisha from the War Office in January 1940 and his exclusion from a Ministry of Information post reveal the continuing weight of anti-semitism. This sentiment in the corridors of power also influenced British Government responses to the wartime fate of European Jews. In the world outside Whitehall and Westminster anti-semitism often appeared in discussions of black-market activity. Moreover, in the course of the German air-attacks on London, Jews faced accusations of aggressively seeking their own protection: this antipathy came on strident display in 1943 at the time of the Bethnal Green tube station disaster which occurred in the course of an air raid. Finally, although the Government interned leading Fascists during the war, some individuals and organizations hostile to Jews remained untouched. Alexander Ratcliffe, whose early hatred of Roman Catholics had become supplemented after 1939 by a fierce hostility towards Jews, stayed at liberty and in pursuit of his anti-semitism became an early 'Revisionist' denying reports of the extermination of Jews in Europe. Ratcliffe dismissed evidence of this tragedy as a Jewish-fabricated plot. The Britons, the organization which in 1920 launched an English edition of *The Protocols* and retained possession of its copyright, did not become a proscribed organization and, consequently, also continued its activities even if it functioned under the ever-watchful eyes of Government and Jewish intelligence agents. Enough has been cited to suggest that George Orwell's contemporary investigation into anti-semitism in wartime Britain reflected more than a personal obsession: it revealed his awareness of the tenacity of opposition towards Jews. The State refused to take any action against this hostility: the internment of Fascists was determined by the wider issue of national security rather than by their anti-semitism.

Although the State refused to outlaw anti-semitic propaganda and activity, it moved decisively against the enemy aliens from central Europe; those refugees who had fled from Nazism, a large number of whom were Jews. Before the start of the war the British Government had concluded that some general internment of this group would be inevitable at an early date. In accordance with this decision the War Office began to reserve accommodation for 18,000 civilian internees and at the start of the war the authorities arrested and interned a number of enemy aliens regarded with suspicion by MI5. Then, on 4 September 1939, the Home Secretary announced a review of all Germans and Austrians living in Britain and the establishment of tribunals to assist in this enquiry. As a result of this categorizing procedure it has been estimated that 528 enemy aliens had been interned by January 1940.

Within a relatively short space of time the internment policy was extended. The Government set up camps across the country and, as in the First World War, the Isle of Man was transformed into a virtual prison island. Important developments in the evolution of policy occurred in the spring of 1940, following the German invasion of Scandinavia and the penetration of the German Army into Western Europe. Mass Observation recorded that following the invasion of Holland anti-alien sentiment in Britain became 'the currency of respectable talk'.[30] In these anxious times voices raised against internment policy carried little weight. By contrast, certain Government departments such as MI5 and the War Office succeeded in raising their profile within the Government and both pressed the necessity of internment. The fact that the coalition Government which Winston Churchill formed in May 1940 following the departure of Neville Chamberlain was anxious to flex its political muscles, assisted the prosecution of their case. Some anti-alien sentiment contained a streak of anti-semitism and a number of the strongest voices urging internment had been sympathetic only a few years earlier to the British Union of Fascists. The internment episode, therefore, can be viewed partly as a continuation of the hostility encountered by the Germans and Austrians before the war when they arrived as refugees from Nazism. In part, the hostility also reflected the tradition of anti-semitism which circulated at both élite and popular levels of British society. Any account which rests content with regarding internment as a touch of 'May madness' is inadequate.[31]

These observations leave unanswered the question of how, after its early stages, the internment policy evolved. By the end of June 1940 virtually all the enemy aliens regarded by the authorities as dangerous had been interned. In practice this meant that, in addition to those of German or Austrian nationality, Italians (who numbered 23,970 in the 1931 census) had to endure the rigours of internment following Italy's intervention in the war on 10 June 1940. After Italy proclaimed its intentions, Italian property in Edinburgh, London and other parts of the country came under attack and it was in this xenophobic atmosphere that Italians, some of whom had flirted with Fascist beliefs in 1930 as Mussolini reached out for his expatriate countrymen, came under the control of the Government's confining hand. Even exiles from Mussolini's Italy, who opposed his Fascist dream, became caught in the net of internment.

It has been estimated, although the figures are of dubious accuracy, that the state interned 22,000 Germans and Austrians; in addition, 4,300 Italians found themselves in the camps. Whatever the reservations experienced by the policy makers in Britain's liberal democracy regarding the restriction of individual liberty, and whatever the quality of the opinion which opposed it, internment had been fully and comprehensively implemented by the early summer of 1940.

Once the programme had been put in place the next stage began in the social control of enemy aliens when the Government, in order to ease the security strain within Britain, introduced its policy of deportation. As a result, the state despatched some 8,000 enemy aliens mainly to Canada and Australia. This programme did not proceed without its share of problems. In one incident the soldiers in charge of the 2,400 aliens on the troopship *Dunera* bound for Australia, robbed and maltreated their human cargo. However, it took the *Arandora Star* incident of 2 July 1940 to bring Government policy under greater critical scrutiny. The luxury liner with its cargo of Germans, Austrians and Italians classified by the authorities as dangerous aliens, was torpedoed, off the west coast of Ireland, with the loss of more than 650 of the internees, the majority of whom were Italians. Following the disaster a public enquiry broadly vindicated the Government but by the time of its publication in December 1940 'the public had turned irreversibly against both deportation and mass internment'.[32]

Surprising as it may seem, in the course of 1940 the Government began to dismantle its internment structure. At the end of July 1940, one month after the last major round-up, a White Paper laid down that certain categories of internee were eligible for release. These grounds widened in the course of the autumn and the process speeded up in 1941 when Churchill became converted to a liberal position. By the end of August 1941 only two camps remained on the Isle of Man: in November 1940 there had been nine. By July 1942 the number of internees had been reduced to three to four hundred. By the end of 1944 a hard core only remained in the camps.

The internment episode and the detention of British nationals under Regulation 18B illustrate that, whatever tensions it might create, in the extreme circumstances of war the liberal state can act decisively against individual liberty. The episode also confirms that in discussing hostility towards refugees the role of the state cannot be ignored.

In view of the extensive curtailment of freedom in wartime Britain, the controls thrown over neutral aliens from Eire should create little surprise. At the outbreak of the war the Government in Eire had indicated its policy of neutrality. This decision needed to be taken into account by the British Government in assessing the possibility of future immigration from Southern Ireland. Workers from Northern Ireland who were coming from a part of the United Kingdom did not constitute a problem.

How did the British resolve the issue of the entry of the Southern Irish, bearing in mind that up to the war no restrictions had ever been placed upon such immigration? Until the fall of France in June 1940 the British Government put no official barriers in the path of travel between Eire and Britain and seasonal agricultural workers continued to arrive without too much difficulty until the spring of 1941. In July of that year, however, the process of movement became formally organized by the British Government in co-operation with the Irish authorities. A number of adjustments to this arrangement occurred later but the only exception to the system of controlled entry came in 1944 during the preparation leading up to D-Day when both Governments stepped in to prevent movement between the two countries.

Over many generations the Irish had filled gaps in the labour market in Britain, finding work in both agriculture and industry. Between 1939 and 1945 it was well recognized that Irish workers could make a vital contribution to the war effort and this awareness in the minds of policy makers triumphed over any residual doubts arising from the immigration of neutral aliens.

But what of the wider public responses towards the Irish? Many corners of the history of the Irish in Britain during the Second World War remain obscure but certain features can be constructed. It is clear that a lingering suspicion towards them persisted throughout the war. The pre-war bombing campaign of the IRA might have been 'poorly prepared and not very effective'[33] but it continued to influence anti-Irish sentiment. Churchill reflected this antipathy in a confidential Admiralty note in 1939 in which he wrote, 'There are plenty of Irish traitors in the Glasgow area . . .'.[34] In this atmosphere the Government prohibited the employment of workers from Eire on the southern coast of England on security grounds and a continuous monitoring of the Irish minority occurred through the trained and prying eyes of Special Branch. Home Intelligence files reporting on the state of morale in wartime Britain also reflected various strands of antipathy. Constant references appear to the anti-British and anti-royalist attitudes of the Irish and their potential danger as a fifth column. Such images sprouted out of the soil of a long-standing nationalist conflict. Echoes of a less politically inspired opposition still sounded in the numerous hostile references to drunk and disorderly Irish workers, described on one occasion as 'the terror of law-abiding citizens in the Leicestershire area' where 'much bad feeling existed towards them'.[35]

These comments appeared in the early uncertain days of the war but antipathy did not disappear as the war progressed and victory became more assured. Allegations relating to the disloyalty of the Irish continued to persist and the long-heard opposition towards Irish workers in the labour market became sharpened by the additional barb that such workers were benefiting from the war when 'our lads' were away at the Front.[36]

A local study of the Irish in Cardiff has suggested that a greater toleration developed during the war. However, the general pattern of responses and, in particular, the difference, if any, between responses towards Southern Irish newcomers and the second generation of Irish descent, remains largely unknown. Even so, sufficient evidence exists on the newcomers to temper any optimistic claims regarding the degree of toleration they encountered.

Wartime Britain assumed a particularly cosmopolitan dimension through the presence of friendly aliens. These groups embraced Czech, Polish, French and Dutch nationals, composed mainly of people in uniform. Between 1939 and 1945 other allies arrived to swell these numbers, as workers and military personnel arrived from the Empire. In focussing specifically upon these imperial minorities can it be assumed that, with Britain engaged in a war on the side of freedom and liberty, a reduction in racial intolerance would occur?

An initial degree of caution is suggested by the depressing report on the economic and social status of 'coloured families' in Liverpool compiled in 1939 by the Liverpool Association for the Welfare of Coloured People. This survey, with its emphasis on the discrimination and disadvantage encountered by long-resident Blacks and their families, provides a sombre introduction against which to consider the lives of those volunteer technicians and trainees who arrived in wartime Britain from the Caribbean. Arnold Watson, a senior Ministry of Labour official, commented in 1942, 'Temporarily at least we have found the pre-requisite industrial conditions. Negroes and Whites can now work in the same shop'.[37] In practice, Watson's optimism notwithstanding, Black workers who came to Britain did not secure a smooth entry into employment. In some firms the management displayed a reluctance to employ Black technicians. A degree of trade union opposition also developed. Fears of labour competition and dilution did not disappear during the war. Even when the technicians secured employment, their problems did not automatically disappear. A succession of complaints relating to rates of pay, the payment of expatriation allowances, and discrimination in working conditions, were heard at the Royal Ordnance factories at Kirkby and Fazackerley.

The difficulties encountered by these technicians and trainees cannot be dismissed as exceptional. The foresters recruited from British Honduras to work in the timber industry also faced racial discrimination during the period of their employment in Scotland. The Government, pursuing the State's self-interest, was prepared to allow the greater employment of Black sailors, as a result of which it not only amended the Special Restriction (Coloured Alien Seamen) Order of 1925, which had created so much tension in Cardiff in the 1930s, but also adopted a more liberal approach to the engagement of stowaways. Even so, Black seamen continued to encounter discrimination. Chinese seamen and sailors from the Indian sub-continent met with similar problems. Some cases filtered through to the National Council for Civil Liberties which fought consistently for such groups throughout the war, but these constituted only a fraction of the problem.

During the war Blacks continued to experience difficulties in the housing market. The Government, aware of potential problems, initially installed the technicians in hostels. Soon, however, some men tried to secure private accommodation and at this point they discovered the strength of racial discrimination. The newly-arrived Blacks also had to contend with a degree of hostility from those such as the Duke of Buccleuch who frowned upon the prospect of inter-racial sexual contact. A number of civil servants involved in administering the scheme involving the Honduran foresters shared this apprehension, as did some of the local population in the areas where the Hondurans settled. Nevertheless, a number of inter-racial marriages provides evidence against an all-pervading antipathy.

The problems faced by the technicians in Lancashire and the foresters in Scotland heaped demoralization and humiliation on the men at the receiving end of such antipathy. However, their problems never gained the degree of publicity achieved by certain other cases of discrimination. The best-known involved Learie Constantine, the celebrated cricketer and welfare officer. On arriving at the Imperial Hotel in London, in July 1943, Constantine, his family and friends, including his Civil Service colleague, Arnold Watson, were permitted only a limited stay by the hotel management, who feared the commercial damage which might be inflicted on their business with white Americans. The irony involved in such discrimination, with Britain engaged in a war in defence of freedom and tolerance, did not escape the attention of David Low who attempted to prick the nation's liberal conscience in one of his most famous cartoons in the *Evening Standard.*

The Constantine case cannot be separated from the presence in war-time Britain of friendly aliens in the form of American military personnel. This American influence can be detected in other situations. One classic case occurred in 1943 when George Roberts, a technician from the Caribbean, was refused entry to the Grafton Dance Hall in Liverpool because the management operated a colour bar in order to placate free-spending white Americans. But not all anti-Black discrimination can be related to the presence of these American allies. The same year witnessed the rejection, as a result of different pressures, of Amelia King, a Black woman who had been born in Britain, when she attempted to enlist in the Women's Land Army. The incident stung Vicky, a Hungarian in exile who was sharply aware of the problems minorities could face, into an incisive visual critique of this incident in which he contrasted King's treatment with the proclaimed war aims of the Allies. Other cases which received less publicity, if any at all, underline still further this discrepancy.

The recent past, 1945 onwards

The opening survey of Blacks and Asians concentrated on the period since 1979. In discussing the years since the Second World War the background to such recent events is open to consideration. However, in examining the years since 1945, it is important to avoid an exclusive concentration on such groups.

The Jewish community, estimated at 450,000 in 1952 and more recently at approximately 400,000 still constitutes a relatively large minority, but little of its post-war history has attracted interest. It is not only the established section of the community which has been neglected. The experiences of newcomers such as the Baghdadi Jews who came from India following the granting of independence, those Jews who arrived from Egypt after the invasion of Suez in 1956, and the refugees who entered from eastern Europe, for example from Hungary, have generated little interest.

Since 1945 the community has become characterized by a greater occupational concentration in the professions and in business. It is also well known that in its politics the Jewish minority in Britain, in common with other communities in the diaspora, has moved significantly towards the Conservative end of the political spectrum. Under the Thatcher governments since 1979 more Jews have entered high political office than under any earlier Prime Minister. These developments have attracted attention, some of which is openly celebratory in tone. By contrast, the Jewish proletariat has been neglected and, in concentrating on Jews and Conservatism, the continuing involvement of Jews in the political Left has been passed over. In addition, celebratory studies which focus upon Jewish success within the context of a liberal Britain, can seriously underestimate the resilience of anti-semitism.

It is often suggested that since 1945 anti-semitism in Britain has been negligible. But is it possible to sustain this confident claim? Events in Palestine, for example, during the last days of the mandate brought pressures to bear on the Jewish community. Has the violence directed against Jews in 1947, in a number of British cities, after the events in the Middle East, already been forgotten? Claims that the 'recoil effect'[38] of the Holocaust and that the presence of Blacks and Asians have shielded Jews from hostility withstand no more than a superficial scrutiny. In the case of racial nationalist groups such as the National Front, anti-semitism has remained the bottom line of their ideology. This is not to claim, however, that anti-semitism has assumed a central political significance in post-war Britain. Nevertheless, it has persisted since 1945 as a species of thought and categorization and Jews have continued to face anti-semitic discrimination. These dimensions are an integral part of recent Anglo-Jewish history. In painting that scene in all its variety of detail it also needs to be emphasized that anti-semitism can quickly revive even after periods of relative quiescence.

The present-day Jewish community contains many descendants of those immigrants who arrived in Britain in the late nineteenth and early twentieth centuries from Russian Poland. After the Second World War Poland also provided the source for another minority. In the course of the war, Britain had offered a refuge for

Polish servicemen who kept alive the 'eagle's spirit' and carried on the struggle against Germany whilst in exile. In 1945, when the hostilities ended, a number of Polish ex-servicemen did not relish the prospect of a return to an uncertain future in Poland where strong Soviet and Polish Communist influences prevailed. At first the British Government urged nevertheless that the Poles should return home. Other pressures soon began to count, however. An adjustment had to be made to the post-war world and labour in Britain remained in short supply. Such considerations weighed heavily on the Labour Government. As a result, in 1946 it established the Polish Resettlement Corps. Through this structure the state intended that Polish ex-servicemen would be directed towards employment and assisted in the process of resettlement. By 1948, it has been claimed, 114,037 Poles had enrolled in the PRC. Nevertheless, the arrangement did not progress without difficulties. For various reasons some Poles did not wish to enrol and the British authorities repatriated a number of ex-servicemen to the British zone in Germany. Among those Polish military personnel who remained in Britain, a reunion with their families from whom they had become separated in the war assumed a major priority. The immediate post-war years therefore witnessed the arrival of dependants, some of whom had been incarcerated in Soviet camps after the Nazi–Soviet pact of 1939 which had resulted in the absorption of the eastern part of Poland into the Soviet Union: after the German invasion of the Soviet Union in 1941 these prisoners had been released. The men formed the Polish 2nd Corps which fought with distinction in the war. The women and children found their way via the Middle East to Africa. From here they made their post-war journey to Britain.

As a result of such developments, Polish communities became established in cities such as London, Edinburgh and Bradford. The size of the Polish community, which in later years gained only marginal increments through immigration, is difficult to unearth from census returns, particularly in view of national boundary changes which affected the country's tortured history, but the 1951 census referred to 161,020 people resident in Britain who had been born in Poland, the majority of whom had arrived since 1945. By 1981 this figure had declined, but the Polish-born population still numbered 93,369.

Discussions of the post-war history of these Poles have tended to strike an optimistic note. Polish men have been described as 'good workers, ratepayers, solid citizens and family men'.[39] Another observer, contemplating attitudes which emerged in Bradford towards newcomers from the Indian sub-continent, emphasized the contrast between the generally hostile responses encountered by these groups and the earlier reception accorded to the Poles and other European refugees who arrived in that city after the Second World War. As ever, any such rose-tinted picture needs to be questioned.

Even though key sectors of the British economy suffered from shortages of labour after 1945, the fear of unemployment which persisted from the inter-war years undoubtedly influenced the reception of the Poles. It intruded into the responses of Britain's miners, for example. In some cases recent experiences compounded this tension in the labour market. Agricultural workers had witnessed the drafting of German and Italian prisoners of war into the countryside and viewed the addition of Polish labour with considerable alarm.

Competition for housing also proved to be a sensitive issue and some opposition assumed a John Bull bluntness. 'How do the people of Liverpool feel when they see these Poles with their new uniforms strutting about our streets, when *our* boys from Burma, heroes from Arnhem, pilots from the Battle of Britain, have to take their wives and families and go squatting? How do they feel when accommodation can be found for these people?'[40] The fact that Polish airmen had fought in the Battle of Britain and Polish paratroopers had struggled in defeat alongside the British at Arnhem, could be conveniently forgotten, if, indeed, it was ever known.

Poles had to contend with a catalogue of other charges. Some were dubbed as Fascists who had fought alongside Hitler, and faced hostility on that account. Certain Poles had indeed thrown in their lot with the Germans and been captured by the British. In viewing the Poles in stereotypical terms popular sentiment did not always maintain a sharp distinction between these Poles and their fellow-countrymen who had fought for the Allies since 1939. In Scotland, where opposition proved particularly strong, the predominantly Catholic Poles fell foul of extreme Protestant opinion which categorized them as no better than 'Papist spies'.[41] Alexander Ratcliffe and John Cormack, fierce opponents of the Catholic Irish during the inter-war years, placed themselves at the forefront of this opposition, thereby continuing their hostility to Poles which had been expressed during the war. The charge which categorized Polish men as 'a race of Casanovas'[42] also persisted from the wartime years. This antipathy, a species of hostility to which male-dominated immigrant and refugee groups have often been exposed, circulated particularly in Scotland but it also stretched south of the border. Accusations of Polish arrogance, an impression derived from the attitudes of formerly well-off Poles who found their new life in exile full of unaccustomed stresses, also became current in the early post-war period.

By the 1980s the Polish refugees attracted less attention. By this time they and their children had become virtually invisible. In terms of encountering overt antipathy and experiencing clear discrimination these Poles and their British-born children fared better than Black and Asian groups. However, the overall picture of their history in exile during the post-war years is more mixed than the evidence drawn exclusively from the 1980s would encourage us to believe.

This emphasis is also relevant to the post-war history of the European Volunteer Workers (EVWs). The demand for labour at the end of the war resulted in the British Government recruiting workers from displaced persons' (DP) camps in Europe. Various national groups had been uprooted by the war which in some cases altered the entire political and social complexion of the countries where these people had been born and grown up. In the DP camps men and women waited uncertainly for a new start, and were hardly fastidious about the type of work they were prepared to undertake, even to the extent of engaging in dangerous espionage activity for the British and Americans.

In these circumstances, with labour shortages in Britain, the authorities proceeded to recruit from the DP camps. Between 1946 and 1949 it has been estimated that the Government imported 91,151 workers from this source. The Balt Cygnet scheme involved the recruitment of women of Latvian, Lithuanian and Estonian nationality to work in sanatoria and tuberculosis hospitals. The Westward Ho! arrangement followed. In this scheme men and women of Balt and Ukrainian nationality arrived from camps in Germany to work in a variety of industries. The British Government also engaged in a number of other less significant recruitment projects.

In recruiting the EVWs the British Government realized that conflict might develop with British workers. One commentator, attempting to put the best gloss on the situation, nevertheless had to acknowledge a certain 'lack of effusion'[43] in their welcome. In fact, in the coalmining industry, a fierce initial opposition developed to their presence from within the miners' union.

In common with many other groups, the EVWs also encountered hostility in the housing market. The majority of the recruits began their new lives in hostels. However, when they moved towards the private housing sector tensions often developed in cities such as Bradford where suggestions began to surface that the Government had assisted the EVWs in the purchase of properties.

Finally, like the Poles, some EVWs faced accusations of collaborating with the Germans during the war. Some of them had indeed served the Reich and the current War Crimes Tribunal enquiry is likely to revive interest in this early allegation and remind us that if, for many years, the EVWs have been largely invisible, for some individuals the history of their reception and treatment might be on the point of a dramatic new turn.

If the introduction of refugees from continental Europe after the Second World War helped to ease existing labour shortages, so did the immigration of the Irish actively recruited by British business firms. Their numbers increased significantly after the war and down to the 1981 census, where they numbered 606,851, the Irish from the Republic remained the largest single immigrant group. It is often suggested that the Irish, well-represented in the populations of London, Birmingham, Liverpool and Glasgow, encountered relatively little hostility during these post-war years, indeed that they experienced a greater toleration than at any other time in their history. In spinning this claim particular emphasis has been laid upon three strands of evidence. First, even if some Irish nationalist activity still occurred, it attracted only a small number of resident Irish and consequently, in contrast to earlier years, did not provide fuel for anti-Irish sentiment. Secondly, it has been claimed that the

Catholic minority, both immigrants and those of Irish descent, benefited from the declining interest in religion. The increasing secularization of society in the twentieth century rendered anti-Catholicism increasingly effete and the violence resulting from such sentiment paled into social insignificance. Thirdly, following the Second World War, the arrival of groups from the West Indies and the Indian sub-continent has constituted one of the major developments in the history of immigration, and it has been argued that the growing presence of these groups, and the amount of hostility they attracted, diverted attention away from the Irish and those of Irish descent.

But how convincing are these optimistic claims? The strength of a widely-diffused anti-Irish sentiment can still be detected in Scotland: it comes on regular display in Glasgow in the clashes surrounding the rivalry between Rangers and Celtic football teams. If the recent signing, in 1989, by Rangers of a well-known Catholic player reveals a break in such tribalism, the expressions of popular hostility to this move indicate the strength of earlier loyalties. Such opposition, a blend of anti-Catholic and anti-Irish sentiment, does not form an isolated example of hostility towards the Irish in Scotland. The sound of anti-Irish-Catholic sentiment echoed in post-war Scottish nationalist circles. This hostility is a powerful reminder that in an age of declining religious faith politics and religion can still fuse together.

It is not only in Scotland that continuing evidence of anti-Irish sentiment can be found after 1945. In England in the 1950s an Irish person seeking lodgings remained likely to encounter discriminatory notices carrying the bleak message 'No coloured. No Irish'.[44] Further evidence of discrimination can be detected in the disproportionate number of recommendations made by British courts in the 1950s and 1960s for the deportation of Irish defendants accused of relatively minor offences. These examples of differential treatment need to be placed against a background of anti-Irish sentiment during these years, the tenacity of which is revealed in a number of sources. One of these is a 1967 Gallup survey which asked the question: 'Do you think that the country has been harmed through immigrants coming to settle here from Ireland?' A high proportion of 'don't knows' prevailed among the respondents but only 16 per cent gave their opinion that the presence of the Irish had been beneficial, whereas 22 per cent believed it had been detrimental.[45]

In the following decade a survey of antipathetic jokes told in the television programme *The Comedians* revealed that anti-Pakistani jokes topped the list, but anti-Irish material came second: such evidence confirmed the continuing strength of the 'thick Paddy' stereotype. By this time the conflict in Northern Ireland helped to fan such sentiment into greater social significance. The majority of the Irish in Britain, as well as that population of Irish descent, kept a low profile on the issue of Irish nationalism, but this calculated response did not prevent the increasing proliferation, from the 1970s, of cartoons, T-shirts and mugs which encapsulated the long tradition of hostility towards the Irish and brought it up to date.

The accumulated evidence on the Irish since the Second World War does not point unequivocally in one direction. The group did not encounter the same degree of hostility as Blacks and Asians, and immigration from the Irish Republic, unlike that from the Commonwealth, never encountered any restrictions. At the same time, hostile attitudes including racialized images of the Irish still persisted, so did discrimination, and, as in earlier times, the most easily tolerated Irish remained those who had renounced their Irishness.

It has been emphasized that the settlement of Poles, EVWs and the Irish is related to the demand for labour in Britain. This fundamental pressure also accounted for the immigration of Blacks from the Caribbean and Asians from the Indian sub-continent, which, in the longer term, as these immigrants created or rebuilt their families, resulted in the growth of Black and Asian minorities. Although the 'pull factor' assumed a major significance in bringing Blacks and Asians to Britain, particularly in the case of immigrants from the Caribbean, other influences need to be taken into account in a rounded picture. These movements can be related in part to the economic problems which prevailed in the West Indies and the Indian sub-continent. Immigrants from the Caribbean tended to originate in those islands which experienced the lowest per capita income. Many of the Sikhs who came from the Punjab in northern India had found their family landholdings adversely affected by the partition of the north of the sub-continent into India and Pakistan. In addition, specific developments such as the destruction of Mangla village in Pakistan when the authorities constructed a hydro-electric dam added to the pressures which generated movement abroad. Other developments also require consideration. Certain British business organizations scoured the Caribbean for labour and assisted the process of removal from the area. In India and Pakistan agents and airline companies helped to grease the wheels of departure and benefited financially from their efforts. Finally, once people had arrived in Britain, whether from the Caribbean or the Indian sub-continent, they assisted the movement of others. Immigration from India and Pakistan in particular became closely linked with village and kinship networks. Through a combination of such interacting pressures individuals began the journey to Britain, a distant country, but one to which they had become linked during the years of colonial and imperial expansion.

Soon after the end of the Second World War some Caribbean Blacks who had been in Britain during the war decided to retrace their steps to the 'mother country'. In taking this decision they added to the small resident Black population in Britain. This group increased further in the late 1940s following the arrival of West Africans, many of whom served as seamen. The symbolic starting point for the more sizeable fresh immigration from the West Indies, however, can be traced to the summer of 1948 with the arrival of the *Empire Windrush*. In the wake of these pioneers who came seeking employment an increase occurred in immigration from the West Indies in the course of the 1950s: these years are the key decade in the history of entry from the Caribbean.

Responses towards Blacks in the immediate post-war years provide evidence of friction, whether the focus is on popular or official responses. In the case of the former, competition for employment quickly emerged as one sensitive issue and, following pressure from the National Union of Seamen, the Government decided in 1949 to block the employment of stowaways. This measure hit hard at the West Africans. In the course of the war stowaways had been tolerated and allowed to work in British ships. Once peace returned, however, the State gave priority to the protection of white workers' interests. Blacks, whether from

Africa or the Caribbean, also encountered discrimination in the letting of property and more generally in their attempts to secure accommodation. In these early post-war years antipathy sometimes boiled over into violence. In Liverpool in August 1948 a group of whites in which an Irish presence can be identified, fought with members of the local Black communities and in the following year, in July 1949, a large crowd of whites besieged a hostel in which newly-arrived Blacks had secured accommodation.

The new arrivals from the Caribbean did not meet any restrictions on entry. The 1948 British Nationality Act guaranteed an open-door policy towards immigration from the Commonwealth. The two classes of British citizen defined in this Act, in other words, the citizens of independent Commonwealth countries and the remainder, designated citizens of the UK and Colonies, were both guaranteed unrestricted entry into the United Kingdom. It is sometimes asserted that this Act, passed by the Labour Government, amounted to no more than a cynical measure aimed at facilitating the supply of much-needed labour. This claim simplifies developments. Within both the Labour Cabinet and the Civil Service disquiet began to circulate as soon as the West Indians arrived. Attlee, the Prime Minister, requested evidence on those responsible for what he called, significantly, 'the incursion'.[46] A similar concern surfaced in the public debate when George Isaacs, the Minister of Labour, told the House, 'I hope no encouragement is given to others to follow their example'.[47] Civil servants, for their part, recognized fully that whereas the EVWs, aliens on contracts, could easily be deported if they became superfluous to labour requirements, the removal of British subjects could not be similarly achieved. Consequently, though senior civil servants adopted a relatively relaxed posture in relation to the recruitment of EVWs, they expressed concern at the arrival of newcomers from the Caribbean. The mandarins also realized that white responses might become a problem. Hence the observation of one official who met a group of early immigrants: 'I am afraid you will have many difficulties'.[48] Some people on board the *Empire Windrush* who had been in Britain during the war might have envisaged difficulties in the future but it is doubtful whether even they realized the extent of the problems they and their children would encounter.

Some of the most significant steps affecting the flow of primary immigration from the Caribbean and the Indian sub-continent occurred later in the 1960s. The Commonwealth Immigrants Act of 1962 initiated an entry system for Commonwealth workers based on vouchers. By restricting the number of vouchers available for the unskilled, the Act reduced the flow of immigrants from the Caribbean and the Indian sub-continent. In the inter-war years an affidavit system operated in Cyprus had restricted the arrival of Cypriots in Britain, but the 1962 Act marked a major change in that legislation passed through the Westminster Parliament to control entry from the Commonwealth. A long tradition of unrestricted immigration for all Commonwealth subjects, enshrined as recently as 1948, in the British Nationality Act, had been decisively overturned. Once the 1962 Act appeared on the statute-book, restraint in matters of immigration control quickly disintegrated. The Labour Party had taken a stand against the 1962 Act but in the summer of 1965 the newly elected Labour Government tightened the screw of control even further by restricting entry vouchers to skilled workers or those immigrants who could be guaranteed employment. These 1962 and 1965 measures placed primary immigration under tight control. However, the 1960s witnessed the imposition of even tougher restrictions in the form of another Commonwealth Immigrants Act passed by Harold Wilson's Labour administration in 1968. This measure was introduced as Asian refugees fleeing from the policy of Africanization in Kenya arrived in Britain. These Asians held British passports, and were 'Citizens of the UK and Colonies'. Under existing legislation they could enter Britain without restriction and, aware that this possibility could result in the arrival of similar groups, the Government decided to close this loophole. The 1968 Act confined the unrestricted right of entry to those Commonwealth citizens who could demonstrate a close ancestral relationship with the United Kingdom. Many Asians such as those in Kenya who claimed UK citizenship through registration at a UK High Commission could not establish any such link. In their case, admission under the 1968 Act became regulated by a quota system, set initially at 1,500 each year.

Why was this series of measures introduced? Why had a decisive break occurred with the tradition of free entry for Commonwealth citizens? The tensions of the early post-war years persisted into the 1950s particularly in the areas of Black and Asian settlement. For much of this decade, however, the opposition to immigration did not secure a strong Parliamentary presence. Nevertheless, a number of interventions did occur. Cyril Osborne, the Tory MP for Louth, provided the Parliamentary focus for such opposition. His was often a lonely stand, but on occasions other members moved in a similar direction. In 1954 John Hynd, the Labour MP for Sheffield Attercliffe, introduced a Bill aimed at restricting Black immigration. However, such activity did not receive support from the leaders of either of the main parties.

Behind the scenes, away from public scrutiny, a different picture can be found. In the summer of 1950 a Cabinet Committee, GEN 325, was established under the chairmanship of the Labour Home Secretary, J. Chuter Ede, to inquire 'whether the time has come to restrict the existing right of any British subject to enter the United Kingdom'.[49] By 1951 the Committee reported that any problems resulting from entry remained localized and restricted to specific areas of settlement. Consequently, it did not recommend the need for legislative controls. The consideration of restrictions by the Cabinet Committee provides clear evidence, however, that public pronouncements by policy makers denying any interest in controls did not provide the most accurate guide to the options then under active consideration within the corridors of power.

The prospect of control did not disappear from the agenda after 1951. Discussion continued on a number of occasions in the 1950s. Apart from ministerial concern over the entry of immigrants, the official papers of the Conservative governments of the 1950s reveal evidence of Ministers' disquiet in related areas. Some Cabinet voices expressed anxiety over the outcome of inter-racial contact. Other issues also feature in the official papers. Churchill, who displayed an obsessive interest in the immigration of West

Indians, instructed the Chancellor of Exchequer, R. A. Butler, to draw up a memorandum on a possible limitation on the recruitment of 'coloured candidates' into the Civil Service.[50] In the event, the memorandum of February 1954 argued against any such development, but it is significant that the issue had been raised.

Immigration control still remained some way in the future and the full range of influences leading to the passing of the Commonwealth Immigrants Act in 1962 remain obscure. The pressures which existed in official circles are especially unclear. It is one occasion when access to government files, which at the present does not extend beyond 1960, would be of great assistance. At the level of popular opinion, however, clear evidence had emerged by 1962 that 'coloured' immigration, as it was called at the time, continued to encounter opposition within the areas of settlement. Hostility also extended beyond these centres. By the late 1950s, the relatively isolated Parliamentary voice of Cyril Osborne had been significantly supplemented, particularly after 1959 when a group of Conservative MPs in favour of immigration control entered the House to represent a number of Birmingham constituencies. Such voices at Westminster, together with those of Labour members in favour of control, cannot be divorced from grass-roots opinion. If MPs helped to channel restrictionist sentiment, they also reflected it. In the summer of 1958 the racial violence which occurred in Nottingham and Notting Hill provided a sharp reminder of developing tensions. So did the less-publicized formation, in 1960, of the Birmingham Immigration Control Association, which acted as a pressure-group for restrictionist sentiment.

Once the 1962 Act entered the statute-book, the restrictionists possessed an additional powerful weapon. The 1962 Act and, to anticipate, the later controls, created and projected an image of Black and Asian immigrants as a social problem and their immigration as an unwelcome development. In other words, official action stigmatized and stereotyped Black and Asian immigrants. As a result, the activities of groups such as the Southall Residents' Association and the English Rights Association received a sharp boost. Although these organizations and other racial nationalist groups could be dismissed as politically peripheral, the return to Parliament of Peter Griffiths as the Tory MP for Smethwick in the 1964 general election could not so easily be brushed aside. In the course of the election campaign some of Griffiths's supporters had exploited the slogan, 'If you want a nigger neighbour vote Labour', and the election result revealed that in certain parts of the country the further control of immigration had become a major political issue. Richard Crossman captured the impact of Smethwick in his diary: 'Ever since the Smethwick election it has been quite clear that immigration can be the greatest political vote loser for the Labour Party if one seems to be permitting a flood of immigrants to come in and blight the central area of our cities'.[51] On the same day Crossman referred to immigration as 'the hottest potato in politics'.[52] The 1965 White Paper on Immigration published by the Labour Government has to be set against this immediate background. Through the Smethwick election the issue of immigration completed the journey from the periphery to the centre of British politics. Labour's stand against the 1962 Act seemed to belong to a different epoch.

The measures of 1962 and 1965 severely restricted the immigration of Blacks and Asians. Nevertheless, restrictionist sentiment remained strong, and by the late 1960s had gathered new sources of strength. The National Front (NF), which on 7 February 1967 welded together a number of disparate racial nationalist groups, constituted one such pressure-group. Clause 8 of the NF's programme emphasized the need to preserve 'our British Native stock' by 'terminating non-white immigration'[53] and until the organization fragmented in the late 1970s this emphasis remained as part of its programme. The various splinter groups which have continued to function following the disintegration of the Front hold to a similar position.

With its racial nationalist links the NF formed part of the British political fringe but its campaign over immigration reflected wider anxieties present in British society. These same tensions acted as a spur to the complex phenomenon known as Powellism. In 1968 Enoch Powell, then Tory MP for Wolverhampton, shot to greater public prominence with a series of speeches beginning in Walsall on 9 February in which he expressed his opposition to the immigration of Blacks and groups drawn from the Indian sub-continent. He insisted particularly upon the potential dangers which flowed from communalism, as manifested in the preservation or re-creation of cultures imported from the sub-continent. The majority of the male pioneers from this part of the world who arrived in the 1950s had intended only a temporary stay in Britain. They aimed to earn sufficient funds to secure a longer term future for themselves and their families in their homelands, to which they would eventually return. The immigration controls of the early 1960s had changed their plans. In these circumstances an increase occurred in the arrival of dependants who came to join the pioneers whilst the opportunity still existed. Whereas many of the men living isolated lives in Britain had not emphasized their various cultures, this reunion of families resulted in an enhancement of religions such as Sikhism. This development met with Powell's fierce opposition.

In the course of his speeches Powell painted a picture in which 'whole areas, towns and parts of England' would be 'occupied by different sections of the immigrant and immigrant-descended population'.[54] In metaphorical and eschatological vein, in his notorious 'River of Blood' speech in 1968, he projected a future in which he saw the River Tiber 'foaming with much blood'.[55] The tenor of these speeches and their rejection of integration, which Roy Jenkins, on first assuming the Home Office portfolio in December 1965, has defined as the mutual tolerance of cultural diversity within a context of equal opportunity, transcended the unspoken limits of the public debate on immigration. As a result, Edward Heath dismissed Powell from the Shadow Conservative Cabinet. Nevertheless, Powell harvested a considerable amount of public support. The clear evidence of racial discrimination directed against Blacks and Asians which had become a prominent feature of British society by the 1960s and the growing expression of physical violence, particularly towards Asian minorities, provide additional confirmation of the vigorous opposition which by now Blacks and Asians had to face and Powellism could exploit.

Against the background of such restrictionist sentiment, which the arrival of the Kenyan Asians further helped to stimulate, and also with an eye towards its political survival, the Labour Government passed the Commonwealth Immigrants Act in 1968. This piece of legislation marked a further retreat from Labour's position on immigration controls in 1962. It can be understood why one anguished Labour MP, commenting on the proposed Act, lamented: 'Have the Government forgotten that this is Human Rights Year? I beg them to remember it. This is not the way to commemorate it'.[56]

Since the early days of immigration from the Caribbean and the Indian sub-continent, a changing body of individuals and organizations had worked on behalf of the immigrants. These forces, influenced by the civil rights movement in America, became particularly visible in the 1960s, by which time a phalanx of liberal opinion widely known as 'the race relations industry', and often closely associated with bodies such as the Institute of Race Relations, had emerged to counteract the swell of restrictionist sentiment. By 1968, however, such liberal forces had suffered a crushing defeat and it is no accident that soon afterwards the Institute of Race Relations fragmented into warring factions.

This predominantly pessimistic scenario might seem to be out of alignment with a number of other developments in the 1960s. For many years Government opinion, based upon legal advice, maintained that the law had no role to play in the protection of racial and ethnic groups whether in regard to discrimination or public libel. The crown did bring a charge against Arnold Leese in 1936, alleging a libel against the Jewish community. However, it lost the case. As a result, it shied away from any further action even when confronted with enormous provocation. In the 1960s, however, two particular items of legislation, the 1965 and 1968 Race Relations Acts, marked important turning points.

This legislation 'was an attempt to influence behaviour and attitudes by [laws] which declared that everyone in Britain was henceforth to be treated on the basis of individual merit, regardless of colour or race'.[57] The 1965 Act established a conciliation machinery in the form of the Race Relations Board, to deal with complaints of discrimination. The Act made it unlawful to discriminate on grounds of race, colour, ethnic or national origin in public places or on public transport. Key areas such as employment and housing, where discrimination undoubtedly occurred, fell outside the scope of the legislation. In the face of continuing evidence on discrimination in these important areas of social life, the 1968 Act was introduced. This stronger measure aimed to prevent discrimination on grounds of colour, race, ethnic or national origin in employment, housing, the provision of goods and services and also in advertisements. The Act endowed the Race Relations Board with power to investigate complaints and, if appropriate, to bring proceedings under the Act. In addition, it set up the Community Relations Commission which assumed responsibility for promoting harmonious race relations and advising the Home Secretary in this area.

In the event, such legislation created little impact. The 1965 and 1968 measures entered the statute-book on the heels of the restrictive immigration controls which occurred in both these years. As a result, the race relations legislation and its related developments did not secure the confidence of many Blacks and Asians. Another defect can be identified. Whereas successive Governments showed a determination to take a hard line on immigration control, little enthusiasm existed behind the surface public relations façade for the legislation on race relations. Consequently, although the developments of 1965 and 1968 can be regarded as historically important, their practical impact remained limited. More than one commentator has cynically viewed the legislation as a smokescreen, the leading result of which has been to provide careers for Blacks and Asians anxious to become involved in the administrative power structure of British society. The observation may be over-harsh but it is nevertheless revealing.

Even though by 1968 a tight system of controls had been thrown over primary immigration from the Caribbean and the Indian-subcontinent, for some sections of British society these restrictions did not grasp the fundamental issue. Among Powellites and within the racial nationalist groups particularly, but also beyond these quarters, the desirability or even the necessity of repatriation was urged. Advocates of this policy could point to history. The Sierra Leone scheme of 1786 and the repatriations which occurred after the collective violence of 1919 provided historical precedents. To those who advocated repatriation the proposal possessed its own logic. Groups from the Caribbean and the Indian sub-continent and, according to some opinion, their British-born descendants, were alien, culturally incompatible with the white British and, as a result, a threat to the nation: as such they should be removed. It is significant, however, that repatriation, whether forced or voluntary, did not become official policy in the 1960s. There were limits beyond which no governments of any political complexion would go.

The important Immigration Act of 1971, passed by Edward Heath's Government, consolidated the legislation of the 1960s. This new measure was introduced by an administration aware of, and responding to, the pressures of popular opinion. Powellism and the National Front were the extreme manifestations of a wider anti-immigrant sentiment circulating in Britain. Neither the new Act nor the various measures of the 1960s which it drew together placed any overt emphasis on the concept of race or on the importance of racial differences. In practice, however, a process of racial categorization lay at the heart of these measures. In the case of the 1971 Act the unimpeded access into Britain of primary immigrants from the Commonwealth became dependent upon the applicant furnishing evidence of patriality, for example through proof that at least one grandparent had been born in the United Kingdom. In addition, the 1971 measure extended the State's powers in relation to expulsion. In its emphasis on patriality, the Act reflected Britain's retreat from the status of an imperial power. As such it continued and brought to fruition a trend which had started with the 1962 Commonwealth Immigrants Act.

The general public cannot be unaware of the debate on immigration from the Caribbean and the Indian sub-continent, but it is doubtful if there exists any widespread awareness of the difficulties which by 1971 faced intending immigrants who did not possess patrial links with the United Kingdom. In part, this lack of awareness might relate to the fact that even after 1971 certain dependants of immigrants already living in Britain possessed a legal right to enter the country even if they did not satisfy patrial status. In practice, this concession often created difficulties which sometimes assumed traumatic dimensions. In the case of individuals from the sub-continent, for example, owing to defects in official records it did not always prove easy or possible to verify family relationships. At the same time, the increased retrospective power assumed by the State following the 1971 Act, over those immigrants who had entered Britain illegally, created additional anguish and at times resulted in the fracture of families.

From the early 1970s onwards public interest has switched away from the process of primary immigration, towards immigrants already living in Britain and their British-born descendants. Evidence on these groups drawn from the 1970s reveals the persistence of the antipathy and relative disadvantage which characterized the years of major primary immigration. A hostility which was 'not merely unverbalized but unconscious'[58] contributed to, even if it could not wholly account for, the difficulties experienced by Black children in education: the level of performance of this group gave grounds for particular concern. Furthermore, the important Political and Economic Planning survey of 1976 revealed the continuing problems facing Blacks and Asians in the labour and housing markets. Finally, violence also continued to be directed towards these groups. Some attacks originated within racial nationalist organizations such as the National Front but in other cases the violence reflected the amorphous persistent hostility towards Blacks and Asians which circulated outside such extreme political groupings. The twisted black and red monument to Altab Ali near Brick Lane, recalling his murder in 1978, is a visible symbol of the violence which pervaded this area of the East End in the 1970s. The monument also serves as a reminder of the racial attacks which continue to be carried out against the East End Bengali population.

An official recognition that difficulties still persisted came in 1976 when the Labour Government passed a third Race Relations Act. This measure abolished the Race Relations Board and the Community Relations Commission and replaced them with the Commission for Racial Equality (CRE). The CRE's intended role was not only to assist individuals who believed they had experienced racial discrimination but also to identify and deal with this social problem. Its remit embraced all the key areas of social life, including employment and housing. The new measure also amended the 1936 Public Order Act and made it a criminal offence to engage in activity which was likely to incite hatred against a racial group.

This Act fitted in with the integrationist tradition which had been established in the 1960s. But by the later 1970s some strands of Conservative opinion had become increasingly concerned about

taking this route. To some extent, this opposition reflected a dis-
inclination to support quangos such as the CRE at the public
expense. More substantially, in an atmosphere in which the post-
Second World War political consensus began to fray, it related to a
growing interest among some Conservatives in defining a coherent
nationalism which often associated nation with race. This development drew strength from the theorizing of a number of intellectuals
such as those who came to be associated with the *Salisbury Review*.
In 1979 these theorists and researchers in various Conservative
'think tanks' found their party returned to power and thereby in a
position to influence the daily lives of Blacks and Asians, and
indeed all immigrant, refugee, and minority groups living in
Britain. The failure of the National Front in the 1979 general
election marks a sharp contrast with this Conservative success. The
NF found itself outflanked by the Conservative Party on the immigration issue. One key development in this marginalization of the
Front occurred in Mrs Thatcher's famous interview in 1978 when
she promised to listen to popular fears on immigration and thereby,
she hoped, bring people back into the Conservative fold. The NF
also underwent a series of internal disputes which possibly reflected
its failure to make increasing political headway. By 1979, certainly,
the prospect of the NF becoming a serious political force, a possibility which could not have been ruled out in the early 1970s, had
evaporated. Down to the late 1970s, however, the Front, along
with the continuing influence of Powellism, which thrived on
issues such as the 1976 Hawley report on Asian immigration and its
allegations of widespread fraud and evasion of immigration controls, helped to racialize the discourse of British politics. In 1979,
following these developments, the question remained: what would
the next decade bring?

This survey has now come full circle. The opening discussion on
the experiences of Blacks and Asians in the Thatcher years isolated
a number of developments which revealed the breakdown of toleration. These ranged from conflict in the employment and housing
markets to clashes over cultural values and assumptions. Some of
this opposition came from organized groups for whom violence
often served as a weapon. Blacks and Asians also found their lives

seriously affected by institutional hostility at both national and local levels. In retracing developments back to 1871 it becomes clear that other groups who did not possess a badge of colour faced similar problems. With this knowledge and information to hand the task now is to probe deeper into the various patterns of hostility which have been identified.

III

Hostility explored

Introduction

According to some commentators, the hostility encountered by immigrants, refugees and minorities reflects a tendency among human beings to prefer 'what is familiar'.[1] Apart from the fact that many people can be attracted to the unfamiliar, this glib explanation avoids a number of issues such as why certain individuals and groups have been exposed to hostility in specific situations at particular times. Other sources have suggested that the roots of hostility lie in 'malevolence'.[2] This assessment is intimately related to the prevailing cultivated image of Britain as a tolerant society. If this 'good' self-image is accepted, then those marginal deviants who do not conform to it can be categorized as evil. However, a discussion conducted exclusively or indeed primarily along such Manichean lines is inadequate. Deficient as a technique for understanding, it is likely to end up as a species of moralizing history. Too much work on newcomers and minorities falls into that category. If explanations such as these are discounted, what can be put in their place?

The role of individuals

The assumption that hostility is a marginal phenomenon has focussed some attention on the role of individuals and the importance of prejudice. This type of analysis deserves consideration, notwithstanding the fact that psychologists and psychiatrists acknowledge that full agreement on the meaning of prejudice is difficult to achieve. Faced with this hurdle, one sociologist has

[65]

remarked that 'it is useless to seek a single definition'.[3] But a working construction is needed. In line with the distinction, outlined earlier, between antipathy and prejudice, the latter might be defined as 'a pattern of hostility in interpersonal relations which is directed towards an entire group or against its individual members: it fulfils a specific irrational function for its bearer'.[4] Such prejudiced individuals, impervious to evidence which contradicts their view of the world, can influence in turn the development of antipathy through their various social activities.

These individuals create their own cave of hatred. One is reminded of Jean-Paul Sartre's comment, borrowed from an earlier German source: 'If the Jew did not exist the anti-semite would invent him'.[5] But if psychologists and psychiatrists can cautiously identify this personality type, is it possible to unearth such individuals from the recesses of the past? Psychohistorians, based principally in America, have advanced our knowledge of the past by applying to it techniques drawn from psychiatry and psychology. However, any historian who endeavours to enter the minds of individuals labours under certain difficulties. Those who are dead cannot be psychoanalysed. Difficulties can also arise with live subjects, when they come under investigation. In any enquiry into the human personality the best and fullest results are obtained when there is full co-operation between the parties. Since many individuals who oppose immigrants, refugees and minority groups would not recognize the need for any personality analysis, there is a major difficulty here. How many members of extreme racial nationalist groups active in the 1980s would be willing to submit to any such exercise? Not that we should assume automatically that these individuals are characterized by the possession of an organic prejudice towards Jews, Blacks and other groups: a survey of National Front members counsels against any such simple proposition.

Nevertheless, some individuals on the fringe of British politics, each of whom revealed a particular hatred of Jews, displayed traits which suggest that their hostility might be related to their personality. It is possible to support this claim by examining the work of Joseph Banister. He was born in St Pancras in 1862 and died in the same borough in 1953. It is doubtful whether many people possessed a familiarity with Banister's outpourings during his lifetime and, since his death, he and his work have been left for the most part in obscurity, temporarily rescued only out of a sense of historical curiosity. Yet for anyone interested in a particularly vicious brand of anti-semitism, Banister's work is an important source. His first recorded comments appeared in 1901 with the private printing of *England under the Jews*. Two more editions appeared by 1907 although the print run probably remained small. The second edition seems to have vanished without trace but the third, fuller than the first, reveals the full extent of Banister's venom against Jews and, indeed, against other groups.

As the title of his major work suggests, Banister's obsession lay with the alleged Jewish domination of British society. He displayed considerable hostility towards established powerful Jews, those whom he termed 'Yiddish money pigs'. However, his vituperation did not stop at this group, but extended to the 'alien immigration plague', or 'semitic sewage', as he referred to it on another occasion, which he saw travelling from the Russian Empire into Britain.[6]

These characteristic references reveal the flavour of Banister's hostility. His work also displayed a morbid obsession with physiology and disease. He claimed that 'the unpopularity of the bath among members of the Wandering Tribe' accounted for the extraordinary extent to which they were susceptible to 'blood and skin diseases'. Jewish blood, Banister stated, 'like that of other Oriental breeds' seemed to be 'loaded with scrofula'.[7] Similar observations lie scattered across the pages of *England under the Jews*, and Banister continued to spit out this form of anti-Jewish venom for the next thirty years or so.

In considering these outpourings, a number of observations are in order. First, whereas Banister's contemporaries tended to mask any trace of anti-Jewish hostility and wrote in coded language – the words 'alien' and 'cosmopolitan' often served as convenient synonyms for 'Jew' – Banister remained unconcerned with such public niceties. He could be equally vitriolic in private correspondence. One wonders how David Soskice reacted in January 1904 after receiving an unsolicited letter from Banister which contained the observation: 'It is a pity that some kind of vermin exterminator could not be invented by which your vile breed could be eliminated'.[8]

Why did Banister display such open hostility? Did he have an inner need to release it? Additional aspects of his work which underline Banister's extremism suggest that he might have needed to hate in order to exist with himself. Three characteristics of his writing are significant in this regard. It should be recognized that stereotypes of immigrants, refugees and minorities can contain both positive and negative qualities, a mixture of 'attractive' and 'unlovely' elements.[9] In short, perceptions can be complex. Banister's hostility, however, continued unrelieved. When he turned to discuss 'the more pleasing points of the Jewish character' he wrote in heavy ironical vein.[10]

Secondly, Banister's image of the Jew can be counted as significant in another respect. Some American writers have suggested that hostility towards Jews has been couched in terms of an objection to Jewish status, power and influence. In Freudian terminology it has assumed the form of an ego-hostility. By contrast, opposition towards Blacks has been characterized by an emphasis on laziness, sexuality, dirt and filth. As such it qualifies in Freudian terms as an expression of id-hostility. Banister's opposition did not fit into this pattern. His hatred towards Jews remained characterized by its comprehensiveness.

Finally, although attention has focussed upon Banister's hostility towards Jews, whether immigrant or British-born, this hatred did not drain all his resources. In a dramatic opening to *England under the Jews* he revealed that his opposition stretched to include virtually every alien group living in Britain. 'Swarms of gambling-house keepers, hotel porters, barbers, "bullies", runaway conscripts, bath attendants, street musicians, criminal bakers, socialists [and] cheap clerks from Germany', alongside 'cooks, waiters, and street walkers' from France as well as 'organists, ice cream poisoners, chestnut vendors, anarchists [and] beggars from Italy', all came under his lash.[11] Among prejudiced anti-semites there is a tendency to 'glorify the "in-group" . . . and to hold strong prejudiced views regarding any and all "out-groups"'.[12] Banister's work supports that observation.

Banister did not stand alone among anti-semites in Britain whose responses suggest the possibility of prejudice related to a personality disturbance. Arnold Leese, founder of the Imperial Fascist League and a fanatical opponent of all Jews, also needs to be considered for inclusion in this category. After he arrived at an 'understanding' of the modern world following his exposure in the late 1920s to *The Protocols of the Elders of Zion*, Leese remained zealous and obsessive in his pursuit of Jews until his death in 1956. He burrowed away frantically into the personal history of public figures in his efforts to detect any Jewish connections, however remote. His belief that Jews committed ritual murder, another claim to which he held unswervingly, encouraged his persistent investigation of murder cases in an attempt to substantiate this article of personal faith. Leese lived in a terrifying world of good and evil, of extreme antipodes, and it is no surprise to learn that after the Second World War he positioned himself at the forefront of the opposition to Black immigration, believing that these immigrants would undermine Britain. This new commitment did not mark any slackening of his opposition to Jews. In the post-Holocaust world Leese never denounced Hitler. He discounted claims that six million Jews had fallen victims to Nazism. At the same time, however, Leese alleged that Hitler's policy towards the Jews had not been vigorously enough pursued. He remained to the end an important carrier of the anti-semitic tradition in Britain.

In a final case study of individuals on the extremist fringe, the spotlight can be shifted onto Alexander Ratcliffe, the founder of the Scottish Protestant League. Ratcliffe's first public career, as the scourge of Catholics and hence the Irish and those of Irish descent in Scotland, reached its peak in the 1930s. It has been observed already that after this point Ratcliffe began to dwell increasingly upon the 'menace' of Jewish influence and that this phase of activity led him to deny the Holocaust. We can now build on these bare details. His pamphlet *The Truth about the Jews!* which appeared in 1943 became a rock for Ratcliffe's continuing interpretation of the Holocaust as a Jewish plot, a view from which he never wavered even when, after the Second World War, more detail became available on the events in Europe. Ratcliffe's anti-semitism also led to his hero-worship of Hitler, a figure before whom the authoritarian Ratcliffe willingly prostrated himself. This anti-Jewish crusade, in the course of which Ratcliffe projected an image of Britain falling under Jewish control, did not result in any rejection or diminution of his anti-Catholic drive. Ratcliffe possessed sufficient reserves of hatred to embrace both groups.

A recent work has counselled against any tendency to categorize Ratcliffe as 'crazy': at the same time, it acknowledged that Ratcliffe 'was not entirely stable'.[13] A degree of 'abnormality' is probably present in many public figures: well-adjusted personalities, it might be argued, have less craving for success and recognition. In the case of Ratcliffe, however, 'Those who knew him admit that he was dogmatic and convinced of his own correctness and virtue to a point approaching paranoia and megalomania'.[14] Virtually everything written by Ratcliffe proclaimed 'the truth' in a fashion which brooked no question or qualification. This intellectual authoritarianism is evident in publications such as *The Truth about Religion in Germany!*, *The Truth about the War!*, *The Truth about Democracy! An Exposure*, all of which, along with *The Truth about the Jews!*, appeared in the Second World War. This authoritarianism ran parallel with crack-ups in Ratcliffe's health which one supporter described, significantly, as 'brainstorms'.[15] This weight of accumulated evidence suggests that Ratcliffe should probably be considered for inclusion in the category of prejudiced personalities.

This discussion of individual psychologies has been taken forward in tentative fashion in view of the difficulties involved in any assessment of figures drawn from among the silent ranks of the dead. Such caution does not imply that the role of individuals in the history of opposition towards immigrants, refugees and minorities is insignificant. Personalities such as Banister and Ratcliffe count among the carriers of hatred. Their activities help to perpetuate a tradition of hostility. In the case of Arnold Leese, any swift dismissal of his role in the history of anti-semitism would be shortsighted. His ideas carried great influence within the National Front and a number of recent Fascist attacks on minorities have been reported by the A. S. Leese Information Bureau.

Marx emphasized that in history individuals matter; they cannot be written out of the script and replaced entirely by impersonal forces. Yet it is appropriate to recall another philosopher's emphasis on the 'intricate web of reciprocal influences' at work in history.[16] To express it another way, the social context of any historical process is of crucial significance. A classic American text on immigration has made a similar pertinent observation. After commenting critically on the view that hostility towards immigrants was largely 'referable to subjective, irrational processes', it went on to argue that 'Perhaps the most fundamental problem for one who seeks a comprehensive understanding of human experience in this area . . . is to find a meaningful balance between the ideas in men's heads and the world outside'.[17] Individuals such as Banister, Ratcliffe and Leese cannot be considered in automatic isolation from the social context in which they had to operate and which also affected the degrees of impact they achieved.

Cultural forces

This final observation encourages a consideration first of all of the social context, defined in its broadest sense, in which hostility developed towards immigrants, refugees and minorities. However, in deciding to travel along this particular analytical route where is the appropriate starting point? A popular newspaper once carried a slogan proclaiming in effect, the past is dead, we live in the present, we believe in the future. But can the past be dismissed so easily? Or is there a need to acknowledge that 'the past is alive, even if transformed in the present'?[18]

If the widespread view of Britain as a tolerant society constitutes one carefully cultivated, celebratory self-portrait, it does not circulate in isolation from other national self-images. A strand of belief emphasizing British superiority over other nations has also taken root. An initial investigation of this theme can concentrate on the emerging historical relationship between Britain and Europe and British perceptions of Europeans.

By the early eighteenth century Britain was already undergoing an important industrial transformation. This process of change gathered increased momentum after 1760 and by the mid-nineteenth century had resulted in the creation of the most sophisticated economy in the world. This transformation, which converted the island country into 'the workshop of the world',[19] almost certainly influenced British perceptions of Europe and Europeans. The country's industrial and commercial development created a need for accounts and interpretations of the world which validated the economic and political aims, aspirations and activities of the British bourgeoisie. It would be unduly restrictive, however, to regard the resulting images of the superior English or British as the creation and possession of that class alone. Through the process of education and various other channels of communication these impressions secured a wider audience.

The emergence of perceptions relating to Europe and Europeans provides only one part of an initial picture. The exploration and colonization undertaken by Europeans in the early modern era encouraged the adoption of images of those groups which passed under European control and influence. By the early eighteenth century Britain had become firmly positioned in the forefront of such expansion and succeeded in toppling France, its great rival, from its position of influence in North America and the Indian sub-continent, and although colonialism resulted in a massive increase in British influence, it did not mark the end of the country's expansion. Historians are prone to describe particular epochs in shorthand, and the late nineteenth century is often called 'the age of imperialism'. The British acquired one third of their Empire and one quarter of the Empire's population in the last quarter of the nineteenth century and this expansion into tropical and sub-tropical areas of the world brought the British into contact with a wide variety of groups.

By the late nineteenth century a widespread interest had developed in race and racial differences and 'the lords of human kind'[20] undertook the work of imperial expansion, the 'civilizing mission', against this background. Once the expansion had occurred, it became widely and frequently justified, particularly on the frontiers of the Empire, in terms of white superiority. The resultant images added to the stereotypes already nurtured in the course of the earlier colonial expansion and which, possibly, had ever deeper roots in European society. These accumulated images were promulgated in many corners of Britain, in school textbooks, comics, advertisements, newspapers, popular novels and in films. The all-pervasive influence of television later became another important conduit.

The notion that the past influences the present provides an opportunity to discuss two other developments. Long before the industrial transformation of Britain stereotypes of Jews had developed and these possessed remarkable durability. In Britain and elsewhere the long historical tradition of antipathy between Christians and Jews had resulted in the latter being portrayed as the killers of Christ, and, as such, deserving of Christian antipathy. From the medieval period onwards this charge had been further refined into the bizarre ritual murder accusation, which alleged that Jews re-enacted the crucifixion through the murder of Christians. Another long-standing and persistent stereotype portrayed the Jews as oppressive money-lenders. They had been shunted into the activity as a result of their status in medieval society as a pariah group, and the resulting obloquy proved tenacious. The pervasiveness of the Shylock image provides ample testimony on this score. Even when money-lending became replaced by increasingly sophisticated financial arrangements, the image did not die, if only because it could be transferred onto the Jew, who was perceived as the personification of finance capital. In this case the stereotype often blended fear with admiration.

It is necessary, finally, to incorporate the Irish into the picture. The reconquest of Ireland in the early modern epoch and Cromwell's suppression of Irish resistance in the seventeenth century had been accompanied by the promotion of anti-Irish sentiment, consistent with the anti-Catholic ethos of the time. As a consequence, 'A great number of civilised Englishmen of the propertied class in the seventeenth century spoke of Irishmen in tones not far removed from those which Nazis used about Slavs or white South Africans use about the original inhabitants of their country. In each case the contempt rationalised a desire to exploit'.[21] Such anti-Irish and anti-Catholic antipathy, which continued to persist, appeared in literature, featured in everyday discourse, and attained a visual form. By the late nineteenth century cartoonists frequently portrayed the Irish as monkeys and this 'simianization' carried a clear message about Irish capacities and attainments. The commonly-drawn link between the Irish and other 'inferior' groups was significantly and graphically presented by Lord Salisbury in 1886 in a speech against the prospect of Home Rule, in which he argued that

the Irish were no more fitted for self-government than the Hot-
tentots.

Although the emergence of these various images can be traced,
there is much less certainty over many of their surrounding details
and influence. Crude popular discourse asserts that 'the wogs begin
at Calais'. But is it possible to refine that feeling of superiority? Did
public opinion in Britain erect a hierarchy of acceptability with
respect to Europeans? Is there evidence of Europeans being
racialized? Were the stereotypes manufactured in Britain characterized by durability or are there signs of change? Did any clear
perceptions of Europeans circulate in Britain? After all, we know
that every foreigner who turned up in Bradford after the Second
World War was likely to be labelled quite indiscriminately as a
'bloody Pole'.[22] Finally, regarding the influence of inherited stereotypes, a sense of British superiority over other Europeans could at
times assist the course of toleration. The open–door policy on alien
immigration which persisted until 1905 is one example of this
effect.

Very little consideration has been given to the 'mutually
antagonistic ethnocentrisms'[23] which developed within Europe,
whereas considerable attention has been paid to the adverse impact
of images drawn from the colonial–imperial period on those groups
who came to Britain from 'beyond the oceans'.[24] This emphasis
appeared in the 1960s among writers who became involved, sometimes temporarily, in the immigration debate. It continues to
feature in the academic literature of the 1980s. But a degree of
caution is called for. After all, it would be wide of the mark to
assume that the colonial–imperial experiences resulted in totally
negative images of the peoples who come under British rule. Certain individuals in Britain, 'felt a sense of obligation towards
coloured people from Commonwealth countries that they did not
feel towards coloured people from non-Commonwealth countries'.[25] Clear signs of this commitment surfaced in 1962 in the
debate on the Commonwealth Immigrants Bill.

Fewer questions have been asked regarding the continuing
impact of inherited stereotypes of Jews, but the most extensive
survey of this issue, which concentrates on the years of high immigration from Russian Poland, is rightly characterized by caution.

After noticing the derogatory cultural connotations attached to the word Jew and the verb 'to Jew', the survey observed, 'it would certainly be unwise to under-estimate the cumulative effect of such usages upon the actual responses to Jews'. At the same time, the survey acknowledged that it was 'difficult to assess such influences'.[26] The same source further underlined this problem when, after discussing common pictorial images of Jews and asking whether working-class people showed any knowledge of them, it could go no further than to state: 'they may well have done'.[27] There is a general point here: working-class images, not only of Jews, but of immigrants, refugees and minorities generally remain elusive. In intellectual circles where an exposure to Jewish stereotypes can be traced more easily, particularly with the growing interest in race in the late nineteenth and early twentieth centuries, even shared images could lead to differing assessments of Jews. J. A. Hobson could write in stereotyped terms of a Jewish genius in finance, express his concern at such activity and condemn its social consequences. By contrast, Alfred Marshall, the Cambridge economist, could write approvingly of the 'special genius' of nearly every branch of 'the Semitic race' in money-making activity.[28] Fewer questions have been asked regarding the persistence of the Jewish stereotype into the late twentieth century. However, a survey of newspaper comment, particularly on Jewish politicians and businessmen, suggests that the hostile concept of the Jew as 'the alien', 'the outsider' and 'the other', in which opposition is often tinged with admiration, still survives, and can embrace even those Jews who have been born in Britain.

In considering inherited stereotypes of the Irish, a degree of caution also remains necessary. A teasing examination of English attitudes towards the Irish between 1780 and 1900 admitted that national stereotypes can be difficult to unearth once we move 'below the level of middle-class commentary'.[29] It suggested also that images of the Irish possessed a more convoluted structure than is often realized. Any emphasis on an over-arching 'anti-Celtic racism' is misplaced: it would be more accurate to recognize that the English constructed a national stereotype of the Irish 'which had both its good points and its bad'.[30] Which of these images became endowed with social significance depended upon other influences such as the psychology of individuals, shifts in religious and other cultures, and the immediate pressures under which individuals and groups found themselves in their relationships with the Irish. Anti-Catholic sentiment directed specifically towards the Irish had certainly diminished by the late twentieth century. However, long-standing negative images of the Irish, stimulated afresh by the troubles in Northern Ireland, including those stereotypes which dehumanized Irish people through the use of animal imagery, still continued to circulate. It would be expecting too much to believe that such representations stuck exclusively to Irish Republicans.

The influence of such immediate pressures calls for further enquiry but before then another set of historical influences requires consideration. Evidence from the Home Intelligence files reveals that during the Second World War the reception of Belgian refugees was influenced by the earlier experience of exiles from Belgium between 1914 and 1918. In other words, contacts within Britain created a collective memory which could assist in the direction of hostility. In certain parts of the country these 'folkways' became transformed into a potent force. In some Protestant areas of Scotland anti-Irish-Catholic sentiment circulated as part of the social coin. It is also significant that some of the speeches made against Jews in the East End of London in the 1930s carried traces of earlier attacks on the Russian Poles. Indeed, an East End vigilantist tradition can be traced over a much longer period. Even so it would be premature to claim that as yet the history of such local traditions has been fully recovered let alone completely understood.

So far, in accounting for hostility weight has been attached to the role of individuals and the influence of historically-generated stereotypes. In neither case can these variables be considered in automatic isolation from each other or from immediate pressures, what American sociologists often call 'situational' influences. These immediate forces now demand attention.

Immediate pressures

This third level of explanation involves initially a consideration of economic issues. The hostility faced by immigrants, refugees and minorities often connected with tensions in the labour and housing markets. In the case of groups such as the Irish in the nineteenth century who were widely perceived by British workers as strike-breakers and undercutters, and Blacks and Asians in the 1980s, attempts have been made to limit and control their employment opportunities. Trade unions shared in this activity. The NSFU campaigns against Chinese seamen before 1914 provide conspicuous evidence on this score. The failure of unions to support strikes by Blacks and Asians in the 1960s is also revealing. Tension in the housing market has proved equally persistent. The opposition encountered by the Russian Poles who came to the East End in the late nineteenth century is now in the distant past but the present-day problems faced by Bangladeshis in Tower Hamlets is a reminder that the housing market remains sensitive. All these conflicts, whether relating to employment or housing, can be centrally and essentially related to competition for society's scarce resources and the power to control their allocation.

Not all competitive pressures can be classed as economic in origin. In numerical terms many immigrant and refugee groups were dominated initially by men and their contact with local women often generated hostility. There is a widespread tendency among men to regard women as a form of property, hence the references to '*our* women', and this assumption, coupled in some cases with the fear that society might be undermined through certain forms of sexual contact, provided the background for some hostility. It featured in the opposition directed towards the Chinese before 1914. Blacks faced it during the violence in Liverpool in 1919. It also contributed to the hostility which Poles encountered during the Second World War and immediately afterwards. During the same years antipathy towards Maltese men often centred upon this issue and popular press exposés which emphasized a link between the Maltese and prostitution proved influential.

The fear, that society might be undermined through inter-racial contact, provides one fragment of a wider cultural anxiety. Strands of this recurring cultural opposition developed within areas of settlement such as the East End of London in the nineteenth century at the time of immigration from Russian Poland and also in the Manningham area of Bradford after the Second World War, when the arrival of Europeans was followed by the settlement of new-comers from the Indian sub-continent. This is not to suggest that cultural opposition turned upon the residence of immigrants, refugees or minorities in a particular area. The travelling gypsies settled nowhere for any length of time but their history is inseparable from an opposition to their culture.

Issues relating to gypsies often featured at the level of national debate and Powellism provides another example of cultural fears securing a national outlet. At all times, in fact, commentators who lived remote from areas of settlement can be found contributing to debates over immigration and cultural change and expressing their fears for the preservation of the social status quo. 'There is a limit to the amount of change that any country can digest at any period', one Conservative journalist claimed, 'a limit after which everything becomes so unrecognizably different that people cease to feel at home; cease to feel that they belong. Alienation of this kind is the death of patriotism since few can love what they do not know or serve what they do not understand'.[31] This sentiment, recorded in the 1960s, still persists. In the 1980s it is directed against 'dangerous' Rastafarians and towards the Muslim claims for separate schools. The recent public debate on *The Satanic Verses* has also raised similar issues in a particularly acute form. Newcomers and minorities in Britain who vigorously and overtly assert the claims of their culture run the risk of counter-attack. The low-profile strategy which many such groups have pursued, in order to survive, reflects an awareness of this situation.

Finally, in the specific case of political cultures, around which anxieties also surfaced, opposition related particularly to what were described as 'un-English' or 'un-British' ideologies and behaviour. An association of some Russian Poles, Germans and Italians in the late nineteenth century with anarchism and socialism led to attacks on immigration by Conservative spokesmen who objected to the entry of such cultures. In the history of the Jewish community, particularly up to 1914 and also during the First World War, any conflict of political interest with sections of British society easily became a fertile context for raising the wider question of the political loyalty of Jews to the nation. The history of the Germans in Britain during the two World Wars also reveals the strength of this issue. As yet it is impossible to say whether the re-unification of Germany will lead to any adverse consequences for the small German community in Britain. However, references in the popular press early in 1990 to the unbridling of 'the old Teutonic lust', and a revival of 'the master race' stereotype, reveal the continuing relationship between political developments and stereotypes, as well as the lingering strength of anti-German sentiment.[32]

An interim summary

In considering the role of individuals, the transmission of cultural stereotypes, and the weight of immediate pressures, the last must be regarded as exercising an especially powerful leverage over responses. But it is worth reiterating that such forces often interact. Hostility develops a particularly sharp edge when immediate pressures and cultural stereotypes inter-connect, as sometimes happened in the case of Chinese and Jewish groups. Furthermore, individuals such as Joseph Banister could draw upon the tradition of anti-semitism which circulated in Britain and capitalize upon the immediate pressures generated by the arrival of Russian Poles in Britain, particularly in East London. Alexander Ratcliffe could draw from the well of anti-Irish and anti-Catholic traditions in Scotland and exploit his material in the course of the inter-war depression in Scotland.

However, such individuals persisted with their hostility in other, less favourable circumstances: their organic hostility did not ultimately require supportive external influences even if their impact on society remained limited by social context. In other words, inter-connectedness does not pervade everywhere at all times. This point can also be made in different fashion. The strength of inherited cultural images could be exploited to direct and justify opposition, in the absence of immediate pressures. In specific terms anti-semitic attitudes can circulate even in societies where there are no Jews.

When considering hostility, the bottom line of such opposition reflects an intention to control power in society and to exclude or confine the power and influence of immigrants, refugees and minorities. In some of the opposition, as when British medical practitioners campaigned to exclude Jewish refugee doctors in the inter-war years and when, after 1945, British miners opposed the employment of Poles, a defence of class interests is clearly at work. However, some responses transcended class divisions. In its opposition to Russian Polish immigration, the British Brothers' League reflected the interests both of some working-class East Enders and of a group of Tory MPs. In more recent times Powell-lism provides a classic case of opposition to immigration embracing a wide cross-section of the public: an analysis in 1968 of Enoch Powell's postbag made the nature of this support abundantly clear.

Local and international influences

In partly retracing, amplifying and expanding the discussion of responses and drawing together the various strands of evidence, a start has been made on moving closer towards an understanding of the various forms of hostility which immigrants, refugees and minorities faced between 1871 and the 1980s. Now that we have gone over three hurdles, in the form of individual attitudes, cultural influences and immediate pressures, and recognized the prospect of their interaction, we have turned towards the home straight, but further challenges still lie ahead and additional questions need to be posed.

Any attempt to establish a close, persistent, automatic link between hostility and national trade-cycle fluctuations would yield little by way of results. However, an awareness of problems in local economies and particular trades can help to shed light on why hostility emerged. The sweating problem in the East End tailoring trade in the late nineteenth century and local difficulties in the engineering industry after 1945 affected the reception of Jews and EVWs respectively. Both groups were perceived as adding to the problems of workers in these industries. Hence the prospect opened up of grass-roots opposition which could be channelled into trade union hostility or, in the case of the Russian Poles, even towards the centre of the political process. The Italians who came to Britain after the end of the Second World War are often regarded as a 'model' immigrant group but they, too, found it impossible to escape from such antipathy. Tensions developed in the South Wales steel industry and also in the coal mines, which led some Italian colliers to leave Britain for Belgium.

An awareness of a broader context of economic and social change can also help to interpret a number of key conflicts. Understanding of the hostility directed towards Germans in the years immediately before the First World War is increased by taking into account the national economic and political rivalry between the two countries. These Germans became caught in the middle of this wider conflict. Responses towards enemy aliens in the two World Wars, similarly, need to be placed within the context of international rivalries. Indeed, since 1871 war has generally acted as a powerful lever influencing the emergence of hostility. At times so has its aftermath. In particular, the anti-alienism in high political circles in Britain in the years following the First World War needs to be set against the loss of national economic power, the transfer of the world's financial centre from London to Wall Street, the fear of Bolshevism following the 1917 Revolution with which Jews were commonly associated, and unrest in the Empire. All these developments assisted the creation of a defensive national posture reflected in the 1919 Aliens Act which had adverse consequences for Jews and even for Chinese aliens who also had to contend with deportation orders. It was no accident that a few years later anti-semitism assumed an increased political significance. The crisis in the world economy had enormous political and social consequences and stimulated the activities of Fascist parties across Europe which exploited anti-semitism as a political weapon. In more recent years it has been acknowledged that the increasing restriction of Black and Asian immigration between 1962 and 1988 and the new definition of citizenship present in the 1981 British Nationality Act came about as Britain turned its back on the Commonwealth and moved closer towards a future in Europe. Finally, the hostility towards Muslims in the late 1980s, continuing into 1990, reflected to some extent a species of liberal and secular opposition in Western Europe to the brand of Islamic fundamentalism emerging in the Middle East and the fears which this religious force engendered. Hence the observation in the midst of the Rushdie affair, 'the rise of Khomeini has rekindled European antagonism to Islam'.[33]

At such times when immigrants, refugees and minorities became caught up in wider conflicts certain individuals could assume a more prominent social profile. Leo Maxse thrived on the developing hatred of all things 'made in Germany' in the years leading up to the First World War. Horatio Bottomley flourished in the fevered atmosphere of that war and its immediate aftermath. Arnold Leese could envision himself as saving Britain from 'the Jewish menace' in the turbulent inter-war years. Enoch Powell's image of England, continually on offer from the late 1960s to the 1980s, provided one view of the new national identity which had to be forged as the retreat began from the Commonwealth ideal.

In presenting their various 'solutions' to society's problems such commentators could draw upon the historical traditions which posited a distinction between 'them' and 'us'. In this vein Oswald Mosley could reduce responsibility for the inter-war crisis to the role of Jewish finance. 'We see [this] enemy and foe, sweating the East and ruining the West, destroying the Indian masses and filling the unemployment queues of Lancashire.'[34] At a stroke immediate economic and social problems became reduced to a single perspective which offered the prospect of 'understanding' to people who had been overwhelmed by the impact of economic movements upon their lives.

The question of numbers

In refining the circumstances which resulted in hostility no consideration has been given as yet to the weight of numbers, the significance of which is often emphasized. In 1891 the *Evening News* complained of 'the foreign flood',[35] associating the problem of immigration from Russian Poland with uncontrollable numbers. Similar sentiment came from William Walker in his evidence before the 1903 Royal Commission on Alien Immigration. In a comment on the Russian Poles he affirmed, 'There is no end to them in Whitechapel and Mile End'. These areas of London, he told the Commissioners, might be called 'Jerusalem'.[36] This claim also featured in the attacks mounted by Major Evans-Gordon, one of the leading spokesmen against immigration from Russian Poland. 'Ten grains of arsenic in a thousand loaves would be unnoticeable and perfectly harmless', the Major intoned, 'but the same amount put into one loaf would kill the whole family that partook of it'.[37] Such pronouncements suggested that the number and concentration of immigrants exercised an important influence over the development of hostility among the local population and even beyond.

The emphasis has been repeated in the later debate on immigration from the Caribbean and the Indian sub-continent. In 1954 one politician alleged that immigrants were 'pouring' into Britain.[38] In the following decade Enoch Powell continued this line of attack, claiming that 'the question of numbers and of the increase in numbers' rested at 'the very heart of the matter'.[39] In 1978 Mrs Thatcher referred to Britain being 'swamped' by immigrants from the New Commonwealth and Pakistan.[40] In the 1980s the image of Britain being overwhelmed is still presented in public debates in spite of the strict controls which limit primary immigration.

It is against this background that the numbers argument achieves a wide currency. In turn, this general awareness further increases the capacity of politicians to play the numbers game. However, the historical relationship between numbers and hostility is less straightforward than is usually assumed. If there is a point beyond which immigration can create economic and social problems, it is not fixed and cannot be predicted with accuracy, whether the concern is with absolute numbers or the concentration of groups in particular localities. Evidence suggests that hostility can be directed against groups of all types and sizes, 'native or new, growing or stationary'.[41] In addition, no conclusive evidence exists to suggest that there is a close correlation between the proportions of any immigrant, refugee or minority population or the rate of its increase, and the development of hostile attitudes towards it.

These general observations might be supported by specific evidence drawn from Britain. Between 1871 and 1914 the largest immigrant group came from Ireland and yet, whatever difficulties the Irish faced, they encountered less hostility than the much smaller group from Russian Poland. This strength of public sentiment relating to the immigration from Eastern Europe led to the setting up of the Royal Commission on Alien Immigration and the passing of the 1905 Aliens Act. Furthermore, in 1911, a small group of Russian Polish Jews in Tredegar had to face one of the major outbreaks of collective violence in recent British history.

A case study drawn from the years before 1914 provides further food for thought. The German gypsies might have numbered no more than a few hundred but they encountered widespread hostility of the fiercest kind. Which other group found itself driven over county boundaries? Which other group did the British authorities deport *en masse* to Europe? The influences leading to the hostility directed against the German gypsies can be pieced together, but the antipathy they faced across the length and breadth of Britain can hardly be related to the size of these travelling groups who sought refuge in Britain from persecution in Europe.

Several post-war developments are also revealing in this regard. Up to the 1981 census, the Irish remained the largest single immigrant group in Britain, but even so they encountered less hostility, whether by way of thought or action, than the newcomers from the Caribbean and the Indian sub-continent. Another observation, relating to the Chinese after the Second World War, is relevant here. As a consequence of immigration, particularly from Hong Kong, the Chinese, who created a powerful centre in Gerrard Street, London, became more numerous than in any earlier period. The latest reliable estimate calculates the ethnic Chinese community at 125,000. Yet the hostility which this group encountered, particularly in take-aways and restaurants, pales into relative insignificance compared with the antipathy which the numerically insignificant group of Chinese faced before 1914. These differing levels of hostility cast further doubt on attempts to draw a neat, one-to-one correspondence between size and levels of hostility. Even so, opponents of immigration have exploited the issue of size to great effect and the tendency of immigrant, refugee and minority groups to concentrate initially in certain localities has provided this opposition with powerful ammunition. In certain circumstances, even small numbers have been made to count as significant. '*They're* moving in on me', a Bradford woman told a visitor to the city in the 1980s. '*A Paki doctor's* buying the house opposite.'[42] Conversely, large numbers alone have not guaranteed the development of hostility.

The question of scapegoats

Not everyone will be surprised at the outcome of this assessment. In opposition to the commonly held view that newcomers and minorities can be held responsible for flooding, swamping, and ultimately overwhelming Britain, another view emphasizes that their role in generating hostility can be discounted. Many socialist writers and historians have projected a general image of such groups as helpless victims who suffer for the crises which are simultaneously regarded as an inextricable part of the history of capitalism. Not that socialists are alone in advancing this type of analysis: many liberal commentators follow a similar critical path in regarding these groups as scapegoats.

Nevertheless, it is important to be on guard against the universal application of crude and simple versions of the scapegoat theory. In a competitive labour market, groups such as the Lithuanians and the Chinese did pose certain problems in the late nineteenth century for British workers just as the Irish had done before them. Weak and disadvantaged groups, desperate for employment, stood exposed to exploitation by coalowners, shipowners and other employers who could use the newcomers to undermine the strength of the indigenous workforce. Hence the observation, relating to the Lithuanians, that 'employers took advantage of the immigrants' poor economic bargaining status to help reduce costs'.[43] Even with the evolution of a stronger trade-union movement and stricter controls over employment practices and wage rates, some EVWs recruited to work in Bradford textile mills soon after the Second World War were replaced at a later date by workers drawn from the Indian sub-continent. In the words of a recent survey, 'It is . . . clear that Asians did replace men in some cases, in particular Eastern European operatives, but they did not replace *English* men'.[44]

The charge directed against immigrants, refugees and minorities which emphasizes their role as competitors in the housing market also requires consideration, rather than being dismissed out of hand. A close examination of the years of high immigration from Russian Poland reveals that although the new arrivals from the Tsar's Empire were themselves often exploited in the East End of

London, their growing numbers, together with the activities of unscrupulous landlords, aggravated the housing situation even if the core defects of the East End housing crisis lay elsewhere. 'It is not without interest that relations [between the immigrants and the locals] seem to have improved as the supply of unoccupied houses increased, in other words as the pressure on housing diminished in intensity.'[45] It is also recognized by some observers that the arrival, after the Second World War, of groups such as the Irish, Blacks and Asians did initially exacerbate the country's housing problem even if, as in earlier years, the infrastructural deficiency had more tangled origins.

In considering the cultural opposition which groups encountered, it would be difficult to deny that certain parts of Britain such as the East End of London, the Leylands district of Leeds, and Bradford, as well as parts of Glasgow and Cardiff witnessed the importation of new cultures, indeed in some cases a succession of such importations, which changed the face of some of Britain's major cities. The transformation of a Huguenot church in Fournier Street in the East End into an orthodox synagogue in 1898 and its functioning since 1977 as a mosque, provide one startling example of continual long-term change. In other cases developments occurred within a short period of time. The disorientation of residents in areas of settlement, expressed in the defence of a well-known and well-worn culture against the strangeness of the new, and the fears expressed by other observers at such changes, need to be considered against such changing cultural landscapes.

Nevertheless, qualifications are required to the interactionist perspective. In particular, it is necessary to scrutinize the significance with which such competitive pressures and changes became endowed. It was easier for white British seamen before the First World War to regard their hardships as a consequence of the employment of Chinese sailors rather than the result of the fierce international competition which prevailed between shipping companies. It was far easier to hold Russian Poles responsible for the housing crisis in the East End than to unearth the complex factors which restricted the supply of residential properties.

Competitive fears and anxieties could also become exaggerated by the widely-held belief that at any time resources remained fixed.

Evidence given to the 1903 Royal Commission on Alien Immigration revealed that this perception affected the reception of the Russian Poles at the turn of the century. A later survey of responses towards the EVWs showed the persistence of this belief. 'There is a vague feeling that there is only a fixed amount of money and goods to be shared and anything given to the foreigner means less for the British.'[46] Even later, in the early 1970s, a similar emphasis appeared in a more general survey of immigration. 'British people whose opinion I asked often revealed a feeling that there was only a fixed quantity of money, work and social benefits to be shared out and that everything for the foreigners somehow meant less for the British.'[47]

The significance accorded to such fears and anxieties was also probably influenced by the constant reiteration of historical stereotypes. It has already been acknowledged that the influence of such images cannot be easily assumed. Nevertheless, the distinction between 'them' and 'us' emphasized by these stereotypes can be related to a defence of '*our* jobs, *our* business and *our* houses',[48] which in turn could nourish an opposition to immigrants, refugees and minorities. Moreover, the related tendency to 'prize our own mode of existence and correspondingly underprize (or actually attack) what seems to us to threaten it'[49] cannot be dismissed from any attempt to explain the various 'them' versus 'us' cultural tensions which developed.

Individuals, groups and political parties also engaged in the exaggeration and manipulation of economic, social and cultural issues for the purpose of political advantage. Some German spies did operate in Britain before 1914 but a general portrayal of the German-born as traitors or potential spies can be dismissed. Leo Maxse's regularly repeated fulminations on this score in the pages of the *National Review* bordered on social paranoia. In the 1930s the British Union of Fascists (BUF) deliberately played its 'Jew card' in East London, ascribing the areas' problems to the presence of Jews. In doing so it hoped to tap the existing opposition to Jews in the East End which had developed particularly during the period of high immigration from Russian Poland. The BUF's campaign was characterized by its exaggerated claims and increasing brutality, both of which reflected a degree of frustration, if not desperation, resulting from the movement's failure to make political headway. In moving forward to the 1950s and 1960s the age-specific fertility rate of Black and Asian women undoubtedly exceeded that of their white contemporaries but the projection of a future in which, towards the end of the twentieth century, 'the urban part of whole towns and cities in Yorkshire, the Midlands and the Home Counties would be preponderantly or exclusively Afro-Asian in population'[50] amounted to a statistical illusion. Yet this allegation, which fastened upon the fear of drowning under the weight of numbers, resided at the centre of Powellism. To concentrate on Powellism alone would nevertheless be too restrictive. From the 1960s to the 1980s, whenever it suited their interests, both Labour and Conservative parties exploited the fears raised by the immigration of Blacks and Asians.

In some cases, the exaggerations of individuals and groups attempting to gain political capital or secure other advantage led to an emphasis on the prospect of domination. The economic, social and political progress achieved by the Jewish community after its emancipation provided the base for the claim that Jews intended to dominate Britain. This message, dwelling on the prospect of national domination, became superseded, following the publication of *The Protocols of the Elders of Zion*, by an emphasis on the prospect of world control by Jews. The first English translation of *The Protocols* to appear in Britain in 1920 carried the significant title, *The Jewish Peril*. This fear of domination also permeated militant Protestant ideology during the inter-war years. In this case, however, the threat was linked to Catholics. The relatively high net birth-rate of the Irish and those of Irish descent in Scotland was forged into a weapon used against such groups. A short-term phenomenon was projected forward Powellite-style, to paint a picture of Scotland controlled by these Catholic forces. In the case of Black and Asian groups the claim has been advanced that their immigration since 1945 placed under permanent siege those 'common loyalties and affections' as well as that 'shared history and memory' which formerly characterized England. As a result, the English had been required to 'disinvent' themselves and were in the course of becoming strangers in their own land. This sombre message, presented in the *Sunday Telegraph* in the summer of 1989, received considerable support from the paper's readership.[51]

Official responses

Some observers believe that the State has played a generally benign role in its relations with newcomers and minorities. However, many accounts of Blacks and Asians in the 1980s have emphasized the weight of institutional racism encountered by these groups in the fields of education, employment, housing and police policy. This discussion can be extended by drawing together and considering further official responses at both national and local levels to a range of groups over a wider period of time.

There is no doubt that in the course of the twentieth century, through a number of decisive legislative developments, the State tightened its control over alien and Commonwealth immigration. In doing so it conceded to, and correspondingly strengthened, anti-immigration sentiment. Historians who concentrate upon a broadening freedom and dwell upon the virtues of the liberal state need to square these assessments with the fact that aliens and many Commonwealth citizens found it more difficult to enter Britain after 1971 than they had in 1871.

Since 1871 the State has also been actively involved in the process of deportation. Numerous examples of this activity can be cited, ranging from the expulsion of the German gypsies in the early twentieth century to the deportation of 'recalcitrant'[52] Poles after the Second World War. Later cases involved Robert Soblen in 1965, and a number of Cypriots who were deported in the 1970s. The affair of Stancu Papusoiu, who was returned to Romania in 1983, and the deportations of a string of Tamil refugees in the 1980s, and Viraj Mendes in 1989, also need to be kept in mind. Up to the late nineteenth century the British State had been more involved in admitting immigrants and refugees than in deporting them. In the course of the twentieth century, however, its involvement not only in immigration control but also in deportation has increased and welfare organizations are convinced that official policy towards refugees has hardened considerably in the course of the 1980s. A number of recent developments reflect this toughness. After 29 May 1985 the British Government obliged Sri Lankan citizens to obtain visas in advance of arrival in the United Kingdom. Never before had any such control been imposed on citizens of a Commonwealth country: the policy was designed to reduce the flow of refugees. Then, in December 1989 the British Government rejected the claim of refugee status advanced by some Vietnamese languishing in camps in Hong Kong, and insisted on their repatriation, with an uncertain future, to Vietnam. This action came under attack from the American Government and also faced fierce criticism at home: nevertheless, the Government persisted with its policy.

Those groups who managed to secure entry to Britain could still not be certain that they would be allowed to pursue their lives free from official interference and control. All aliens remained ineligible for positions in the armed forces and the Civil Service. The reasoning behind such restrictions can be appreciated. It is more difficult to comprehend why official restraints continued to limit the career choices of their British-born children. The status transition from an alien to a British subject could be achieved of course through the process of naturalization. However, this transformation did not always proceed without difficulty. To be more precise, there is evidence in Home Office files compiled in the 1920s to suggest that officials placed obstacles in the path of Russian Polish Jews applying for naturalization.

Immigrants from the Commonwealth were British subjects. As such, it would have been impossible to impose official legal restrictions on them. Nevertheless, abundant evidence can be found of *de facto* discrimination, perhaps the most notorious example of which came with the treatment of Black British sailors in Cardiff by the local police in the inter-war years. This episode is a reminder that tensions between inner-city minorities and the police in the 1980s had earlier parallels. The events in Cardiff also illustrate the importance of studying local contexts and suggest regional variations in responses.

All these developments along with other issues, such as the internment episodes of the two World Wars, qualify the image of a tolerant, benign state. Some writers have been particularly anxious to develop this perspective as one part of a bigger, sustained attack upon the perceived rottenness of a society they consider to be ripe only for deserved destruction. However, it makes sense to hesitate before accepting all their arguments. At both central and local levels, official responses provided evidence of another face. Before 1914 the police in Liverpool helped to dampen the claim that the Chinese constituted a social problem. In the First World War the State assumed responsibility for the daily lives of the 200,000 Belgian refugees. Without this intervention, these Belgians would have faced serious difficulties and could have encountered greater hostility. In 1919 the police in Liverpool helped to shield Blacks against the White collective violence which raged in the city. Finally, whatever its well-rehearsed defects, the race relations legislation passed in 1965 and 1968 and the currently valid act of 1976 marked the State's first faltering steps to prevent discrimination on grounds of race.

In general, groups were more likely to be officially tolerated when their interests were perceived by the State to be in alignment with its own. By contrast, those viewed as having interests antithetical to the State or superfluous to its requirements could be particularly exposed, especially during periods of significant social change: any such groups under-represented in the official power-structure could be viewed as undeniably vulnerable.

Ambiguity and ambivalence

In isolating the various forms of official opposition to immigrants, refugees and minorities there is yet another avenue which calls for exploration. It is relatively easy to spot overt forms of opposition but more subtle, less apparent forms of opposition, dressed up, in some cases, as expressions of liberal toleration are less easy to detect. The history of Jewish emancipation is instructive in this sense. By the late nineteenth century Jews had finally become emancipated, even though this policy had run into greater opposition than the campaigns which lifted restrictions from Roman Catholics and Unitarians. On the surface, the eventual emancipation of the Jews can be represented as one example of the widening toleration of religious minorities and a classic example of Liberalism in action. However, Jewish emancipation was regarded in Parliament as a contract which assumed that Jews would cease to regard themselves primarily as Jews. In other words, the emancipation process can be viewed as possessing its own strand of intolerance. Official attitudes towards other groups have revealed a similar ambiguous pattern. The same notion of 'contract' unwritten but understood, has continued to influence official responses since the Second World War towards Polish and Irish groups. Furthermore, gypsies have often been confronted by local authorities anxious 'to pose as the champions of freedom and Gypsy culture, while in fact trying to suppress it'.[53] Such ambiguity resided within the 1968 Caravan Sites Act which appeared in the guise of a liberal measure. However, gypsies viewed it differently. They regarded it as a piece of legislation which 'was equated with settlement, and in turn equated with assimilation'.[54] A surface liberalism carried beneath its façade traces of the long-standing cultural antipathy which gypsies in Britain had to face along with the travelling people of other countries.

A transfer of emphasis from the official world to general public opinion reveals the presence of similar complex structures. It has been recognized that, in the midst of hostility immigrants, refugees and minorities found their defenders. However, a clear, sharp fracture cannot always be found between positive and negative responses: on the contrary, a degree of ambivalence can often be identified. Hence 'Chips' Channon, although a great friend of Leslie Hore-Belisha, could still refer to Belisha in a term redolent of the time, as 'the Jew boy'. This comment was followed by the remark '[but] I am fond of him'.[55] A similar complexity can be found in Mass Observation surveys where it is not uncommon to find respondents making contrasts between intelligent Jews such as Sigmund Freud and 'fat, greasy, assertive second hand Jews'.[56] Such observations underscore the fact that perceptions are not always one-dimensional: individuals are capable of combining both positive and negative images or, in another historian's words, 'Even the supposedly inflexible sort of judgement which the ethnic stereotype represents can incongruously combine both positive and negative charges'.[57]

In claiming that the face of hostility does not have to be constantly set in one mould but can display a variety of expressions, there is no reason to concentrate exclusively on attitudes towards Jews. 'The present day pattern of employment of Irish labour', an observer wrote in 1963, 'still shows something of the characteristically ambivalent British attitudes towards the Irish both by employers and fellow workers.' The writer then expanded his observation: 'Their labour may be appreciated and fellow workers may accept them quite readily but an undertone of doubt is likely to remain to suggest that the Irish because they are Irish are likely to prove unsatisfactory or a potential danger.'[58]

Similar 'split' attitudes can be detected in the responses which greeted those Poles and Ukrainians who settled in Bradford after the Second World War. Furthermore, early in 1990, in the debate over the possible entry of people from Hong Kong, which resulted eventually in 50,000 Hong Kong Chinese, their spouses and children being granted the right of abode in the United Kingdom, Chinese men were positively stereotyped as thrusting, efficient businessmen, and the group as a whole secured praise for its devotion to family life. However, alongside these stereotyped traits, the same observers drew critical attention to the tendency of the Chinese to cling tenaciously to their own culture, and also to the group's inclination to opt out of its wider social responsibilities.

Finally, a range of responses towards Blacks in twentieth-century Britain can be marshalled to reveal hostility lurking behind a surface sympathy. This mixture can be detected in the ideology of 'philanthropic racism'[59] which Blacks encountered both from individuals and organizations allegedly concerned with their welfare. Furthermore, the Conservative Party's attempt, in the 1983 general election, to capture the vote of upwardly mobile Blacks might seem on the surface to be a generous extension of Conservatism. Below that surface, however, the poster, 'Labour says he's Black, Tories say he's British' suggested a rejection of those Blacks who clung to any fragment of their cultural distinctiveness. White observers failed to spell out the full implication of the poster: Black commentators showed a greater awareness of the nature of the offer.

A similar ambivalence can be found if the centre of interest shifts from thought to behaviour. 'You can be the best of buddies with someone during the day but when it's night-time, forget it.'[60] This comment by a Black soldier in the American army finds parallels in Britain, with groups being tolerated in specific situations where they were not perceived as a threat. Gypsies can relate a long history in which they have been tolerated as entertainers whilst encountering widespread hostility wherever they moved. In the late nineteenth and early twentieth centuries money-making skills among Jews could be tolerated , or even praised, but beyond such conformity to 'the values and manners of bourgeois English society'[61] they were often crudely and sometimes subtly discriminated against as Jews. The Polish refugees who stayed in Britain after 1945 encountered similar ambivalent treatment. They could be turned out of an NCB hostel in Scotland in 1947 in the belief that such accommodation should be reserved for native Scots. However, in the world of Scottish football, some Polish players became local idols. In the case of Blacks they, like gypsies, have been widely but not universally tolerated throughout the modern epoch as entertainers, but rejected once they left that small world. Prominent in sport in the 1980s, although still strikingly absent in the Yorkshire cricket eleven, Black athletes found it difficult nevertheless to enter the administrative side of their sporting activities. First-class athletes could remain consigned to second-class citizenship. The comments of a Liverpool taxi driver help to bring home the practice of variable treatment: 'I can take them or leave them the same as anybody else you know. I don't mind having a drink with a coloured chap. I've met some very nice coloured people but with regard to intermarriage I think I'd draw the line there'.[62]

Concluding comment

In reflecting on the pattern of responses, there might be a temptation to draw the conclusion that European groups have fared better than those newcomers and minorities who came from further afield. In defence of this position it might be pointed out that after 1945 Jewish and Irish groups have faced less hostility than Blacks and Asians: examples of discrimination and collective violence directed against the two former, for example, are less in evidence. But a wider sweep of history soon reveals the dangers of any such generalization. Before 1914 two European groups, the Russian Polish Jews and the German gypsies, experienced far more hostility than any of the imperial groups living in Britain at that time.

Confident claims regarding the position of particular groups also need to bear in mind that sudden shifts can occur in perceptions and treatment. The rapid deterioration in the position of the so-called 'Court Jews' of German origin, as Britain and Germany moved towards war, and, at a later date, the drastic change in the fortunes of the Italians following the entry of Italy into the Second World War, reveal the fragility of toleration. Furthermore, although as yet the answer must remain uncertain, it is worth reflecting on the consequences which the immigration of Chinese from Hong Kong after 1997 might have on the established Chinese community in Britain: spokesmen in London's Chinatown have already expressed some anxiety on this score.

There is a need to be particularly wary of claims that immigrants, refugees and minorities can become 'safe' as a result of hostility being aimed at other groups. This suggestion is specious and dangerous. Hostility is not a fixed quantity and there is no evidence to suggest that if it is transmitted in one direction there are insufficient reserves left over for other groups. The National Front has found no difficulty in attacking Blacks and Asians but, at the same time, keeping anti-semitism at the centre of its ideology.

In the light of these observations, and the earlier emphasis on ambiguity and ambivalence, with hostility varying from situation to situation and from context to context, the complexity of responses becomes more apparent. This observation is further underlined if due weight is attached to the noticed variations in hostility between areas: the Chinese fared better in Liverpool than in Cardiff before 1914 because of structural differences in the shipping industry. Hostility towards the Irish, as well as the Poles, has also revealed variations related to specific local pressures and traditions.

One final observation is now worthwhile. Contrary to what is often thought, there is no evidence that immigrants, refugees and minorities of whatever race or nationality always follow a path from an initial rejection to a subsequent acceptance or toleration. Hostility towards such groups sleeps lightly. In such circumstances they have every reason to remain eternally vigilant and search for strategies which might offer a cushion against opposition. In some cases, in an attempt to avoid labour market pressures, this has resulted in an emphasis on self-employment, a policy pursued by many groups including the Chinese, Cypriots, Italians, Jews and Pakistanis. In other instances it has encouraged efforts to secure safety through an involvement with the labour movement. This connection assisted the organization of immigrant workers and thereby helped to modify their image as cheap fodder for employers: it provided also an institutional bulwark against opposition. Such developments have been stressed particularly in accounting for the status of the Irish in Scotland. In many cases representatives of the newcomers and minorities have urged the need for an accommodation with the majority of the cultural norms in Britain in order to avoid 'visibility' and a possible exposure to hostility. However, whatever benefits have resulted for particular groups, at specific times, none of these strategies has guaranteed an unbroken sense of security or provided a permanent barrier against opposition. In short, there have been no immutable hierarchies of acceptance or toleration, whether of individuals or groups.

IV

Conclusion

The history of recent immigration into Britain is surrounded by myths. It is sometimes claimed that there is no tradition of immigration. Useful as this assertion might be as a tool for the policy-maker anxious to restrict entry, it has no substantial historical basis. Indeed, 'the British are clearly among the most ethnically composite of the Europeans'.[1] A concentration on the years since 1871 has yielded abundant evidence on immigration as a continual process and an extended survey, covering earlier years, would reveal a similar trend. Nevertheless, this observation calls for qualification.

Whatever the levels of recent movement into Britain, they never reached the scale of entry into America. From the late nineteenth century, America became the world's major magnet for immigrants and refugees, drawing to itself not merely newcomers from northern and western Europe, as in the early nineteenth century, but an increasing number of immigrants and refugees from southern and eastern Europe and a growing population from Asia, including Chinese and Japanese. The varied ethnic mix of present-day America reveals the extent to which immigration has been a major feature of American development.

International comparisons aside, any image of Britain as an importer of population requires further qualification. Opponents of immigration since 1871 have not been slow to draw the narrow picture of Britain as a small, over-crowded island which faced the prospect of being overwhelmed by hordes of newcomers. The seas surrounding the British Isles have long been perceived as possessing a defensive quality: to cite one instance only, Burke's 'slender dyke'[2] has been widely regarded as a safeguard against invasion from the Continent. But imagery related to the seas has been a widespread feature of anti-immigration sentiment. Hence the frequent references to the 'flood' of newcomers, described as arriving in 'waves' and subsequently 'swamping' British society.[3] These images suppress the fact that in virtually every year since 1871 Britain has been a net exporter of population. This crucial fragment of statistical evidence needs to be kept firmly in mind in any discussion of recent immigration. Even so, an awareness of it does not invalidate the claim that Britain has provided a base, whether temporary or permanent, for a continual flow of immigrants and refugees. A failure to recognize this development and, furthermore, to take account of its implications, diminishes any attempt to understand recent British history.

In contrast to the general lack of knowledge regarding the tradition of immigration in British history, a widespread view circulates that groups who did arrive were generally tolerated. Indeed, if only because it helps to puff up national pride, an emphasis upon Britain as a centre of liberty and toleration is the starting point for many discussions of immigrants, refugees, and minority groups.

Some indication of the widespread public expression of such sentiment has already been provided but it deserves to be extended. Apart from the emphasis on a national tradition of toleration, a claim has been submitted for its vitality in certain areas where immigrants and refugees have settled in recent years. 'It would require long and careful investigation to establish the claim that Manchester has absorbed a rare tradition of tolerance towards strangers and foreigners consistent with the great liberal traditions of trade and politics of which nineteenth century Mancunians were so proud', a history of the city lengthily proclaimed, but 'the general treatment of immigrants seems to redound to the city's credit'.[4] By the nineteenth century Manchester had already assumed the character of a cosmopolitan city: its industrial and commercial developments attracted a diverse range of immigrants. Any reference to the settlement of immigrants and refugees would nevertheless suggest to many people a link with the East End of London. A succession of different newcomers have trodden its streets and, reflecting on this process, Ian Mikardo, who recently represented the Bow and Poplar constituency, emphasized the toleration with which they had been received. 'The majority of

East Enders are kindly and tolerant towards those around them whoever they are and wherever they come from', he wrote in 1982, and suggested that this toleration derived from 'a sense of solidarity among people struggling to earn a living and maintain decent standards'.[5] It is a remark which jars on the ears of those who have probed beneath the surface of East End social life. Nevertheless, the drift of such celebratory comment is particularly significant and often heard. By heaping responsibility for any contrary behaviour upon an irresponsible fragment of society, the illusion of the essential decency and toleration of the rest of the population can be preserved.

Those observers who promote the image of a tolerant Britain are assisted by comments emanating from immigrants and refugees. In the nineteenth century that well-known anarchist, Peter Kropotkin, recalled his thoughts at the time of his expulsion from Europe. 'As I went to the steamer', he wrote, 'I asked myself with anxiety "Under which flag does she sail – Norwegian, German, English?" Then I saw floating above the stern the union jack – the flag under which so many refugees, Russian, Italian, French, Hungarian, and of all nations have found an asylum. I greeted that flag from the depth of my heart'.[6] Kropotkin's comments have been echoed by other newcomers. The impressions left by Peppino Leoni, the Italian restaurateur, whose business success began in the 1920s, and the autobiography of the more obscure Wallace Collins, an immigrant from Jamaica, whose recollections appeared in 1965, help to support the image of Britain as a tolerant country. Such testimony might be rounded off with a couple of more recent observations. A letter in a Bradford newspaper in 1984 under the heading, 'A paradise with shops full of food', emphasized that 'coming from a Communist country and from war slave camps in Germany we thought and still think, England and Bradford is a paradise'.[7] Finally, in his maiden speech in the House of Lords in 1988 Lord Jakobovits, the Chief Rabbi, helped to sustain this tolerant image when he reminded their Lordships that 'but for the grace of God and the compassionate haven of this great country I should today be an anonymous speck among the ashes of millions defiling the soil of Europe'.[8]

These comments from Bradford and Westminster draw attention

to the fact that toleration possesses a relative as well as an absolute dimension. This issue will be considered in a moment, but at this juncture a summary of the existing discussion is needed. The essence of the argument can be summarized briefly along the following lines. Hostility did not occur at all times, on all occasions, against all groups. The diversity of responses has been recognized. However, even if opposition was not universally persistent, the cumulative evidence of expressions of hostility cannot be ignored. In considering the years from 1871 onwards, opposition surfaced at the level of ideas, whether in spoken or written form. It resulted sometimes in discrimination. It influenced outbreaks of collective violence. The weight of such evidence qualifies the widely-held view of Britain as a tolerant country. There is relevance in Hannah Arendt's observation that 'we can no longer afford to take that which was good in the past and simply call it our heritage, to discard the bad and simply to think of it as a dead load which by itself time will bury in oblivion'.[9]

Apart from providing evidence on the tenacity of hostility, an attempt has been made to understand such opposition. In pursuing this goal, an emphasis has been placed on the role of individuals: at particular times certain figures have been in the vanguard of opposition. Their role needs to be accorded a degree of prominence, but an exclusive concentration upon this dimension does not bring us to the heart of the problem. A fuller understanding of it becomes possible when the focus is shifted from individuals towards a consideration of the social context, broadly defined, in which hostility occurred, from which such individuals could draw support and in which they functioned most effectively.

In order to understand that context an awareness is needed of the influence of historically based stereotypes which are constantly being created and renewed, including images which have developed in the course of contact in Britain. Even so, the precise influence of such stereotypes is difficult to pin down. Nevertheless, the past cannot be totally excluded from an interaction with the present and in considering the latter, an emphasis has been placed upon hostility arising particularly from competition for jobs and housing, but conflict arising from sexual relationships has been emphasized as another important immediate pressure. Finally, any consideration of immediate or situational pressures, bearing in mind the significance of specific local influences, soon provides a sharp reminder that man does not live by bread alone. There is abundant evidence of tensions relating to a clash of cultures both secular and sacred. These immediate pressures exercised a powerful leverage over responses, in the course of which historical stereotypes could be drawn upon to great effect. All such opposition can be related ultimately to the control of power and influence. At times it reflected a defence of class interests but responses can be traced which transcended class divisions.

This emphasis on the often interacting influences of individuals, historical conditioning, and immediate competitive pressures, has been placed at the centre of the attempt to understand why hostility occurred. It has been suggested additionally that a close, persistent and automatic link between such opposition and downturns in the national economy cannot be detected. However, sectoral and local fluctuations as well as broader patterns of social-economic change have provided a fertile context for the development of tensions. At the same time, a question mark has been placed against any one-to-one correlation between the size of immigrant, refugee or minority groups and the development of conflict. Furthermore, a warning shot has been sounded against dismissing all the opposition encountered by such groups as no more than a reflection of the fantasies of those who opposed them. Yet it has also been recognized that the charges they faced have been susceptible to distortion and that certain issues have been exploited for political ends.

On enquiring specifically into official attitudes and behaviour at both national and local levels it becomes clear that alongside positive interventions it is possible to trace various examples of overt antipathy which call into question the widely-held image of the benign state. At the same time, various thrusts of official policy dressed up in liberal garb, and accepted as such, can be revealed as possessing a less generous aspect when stripped down to their essential core. This evidence, multiplied in the attitudes and behaviour of individuals and groups, suggests a need to be vigilant regarding the varied forms which hostility assumed and the degree of ambiguity and ambivalence present in attitudes and behaviour. It might be a type of reassurance to advance simple explanations of hostility and such simplicity is often used for political ends. However, those travelling along this route need to be brought face to face with its limitations. In studying hostility we enter a territory which needs to be tamed in order to be understood.

In pursuing this tougher and tighter explanation of hostility two concepts have been treated with caution. References to prejudice slip easily into the currency of everyday conversation in spite of the fact that there is no 'consensual agreement' among specialists on its definition.[10] A strong case can be made for restricting its use to the inflexible hostile attitudes of those individuals with a personality disturbance to which their hatred is inextricably linked. If this case is accepted, a term is still required for that hostility, displayed by those lacking any discernible personality disturbance, which ebbs and flows within individuals and groups according to changing circumstances. The bulk of the hostility which has been identified falls into this category. It has been labelled as antipathy. This conceptual distinction is not absolute in the sense that prejudiced individuals can influence the development of antipathy, but neither is it purely semantic; it allows a sharper distinction to be made between various types of hostility and carries policy implications.

The second concept on which a warning note should be sounded is racism. Many commentators, politicians, journalists and academics, sprinkle references to racism and racists into their observations on Britain's Black and Asian minorities. In April 1988, for example, one Black member of Parliament accused Britain of being 'one of the most fundamentally racist nations on earth'.[11] Some movement has also occurred in the other direction. In the same month, the Home Secretary denounced the 'new hatred of Britain's black racists' whom he accused of 'being just as prejudiced as white bigots'.[12] Academics, too, have drawn heavily upon racism in their accounts of recent developments. Typical of this usage is the comment in 1975 in a popular introductory text: 'The racist position on race has achieved respectability in about ten years'.[13] These observations seldom carry any recognition that racism and its derivatives possess a complex history and few who use the terms display any inclination to offer a definition of their concepts in order to assist an understanding of their discourse.

If racism is defined as a doctrine which posits the existence of inherent biological or genetic differences between racial groups, and claims that such differences allow for a grading and ranking of groups as superior or inferior in capacities, capabilities and attainments, then there is abundant evidence of such sentiment in Europe after 1871. In the late nineteenth and early twentieth centuries it can be viewed in fact as 'an integral part of the European experience'.[14]

A comprehensive history of racism in Britain remains to be written but after 1871 strands of hostility in Britain which reflected a belief in biological differences and associated cultural and moral traits can be found. In the pre-1914 debate on Russian Polish immigration such sentiment loomed large and striking in the outpourings of Joseph Banister, it featured in the journalism of J. L. Silver in the *Eastern Post and City Chronicle* and appeared in the writing which emerged in eugenics circles. After 1914 it revealed itself in the work of Karl Pearson and featured in Arnold Leese's opposition to Jews all of whom he perceived as Asiatics intent on undermining Nordic civilization. Some of the hostility encountered by the Irish in the nineteenth century contained similar racialized images and G. R. Gair's opposition in Liverpool in the 1930s to the so-called 'Mediterranean Irish', also presented as an inevitable threat to Nordic civilization, continued this tradition. Such opposition, communicated with varying degrees of sophistication, nudges us into recognizing that biological racism is not a badge of oppression which is fastened on Blacks and Asians alone. However, it is better known that since the Second World War a similar type of opposition has been faced by Black and Asian immigrants and their decendants. After the collective violence in 1958 in Nottingham and Notting Hill, a pamphlet issued by the Eugenics Society emphasized the importance of fundamental racial differences and counselled against a liberal approach to immigration. Finally, any reader of *Spearhead*, the National Front publication, during the political heyday of the NF in the 1970s could hardly avoid the persistent emphasis, replete with sexist imagery, on the damage and decay which allegedly followed from miscegenation. This note of biological racism still continues to sound in racial nationalist circles.

However, racism is not always defined in biological terms. It is widely argued that since the end of the Second World War such overt opposition has become modified in the shadow of the Holocaust, and that any definition of racism needs to take account of this shift, and the corresponding emergence of 'functional equivalents' to biological racism. To put it differently, a sensitivity is needed to other species of deterministic categorization which 'might be based upon religious, cultural, historical, ideological or sociological grounds and . . . might be more or less adequately placed in a systematic theory of an explicit kind'. In other words the cultural opposition encountered by groups such as the Irish, the Jews, the Germans, the Poles, the Blacks and the Asians, which, even though it did not carry any biological or genetic emphases, still nevertheless maintained that 'this man is an X and that being an X, he is bound to have undesirable qualities', is a form of racism.[15] In this shape racism undoubtedly seeps into public opinion: hence the ease with which the execution of *The Observer* journalist, Farzad Bazoft, in Iraq in 1990 could be dismissed quite quickly in some circles because he was a Middle Easterner, 'Not a white man, not one of us'.[16] A further dimension can be added to these layers of emphasis: since the late 1960s racism has become widely regarded not so much as a doctrine but as a structural phenomenon present within and operating out of institutional frameworks. In other words, there has been a growing recognition of the importance of institutional racism. More recently still, since 1981, some emphasis has been placed upon 'the new racism' and its insistence on the 'naturalness' of opposition towards minorities, 'the others', in view of the instinctive tendency of human nature to defend traditions and customs against outsiders.

What is the upshot of all this discussion? It is becoming clear that definitions and emphases can change over a period of time and that racism possesses its own history. Some writers have recognized the potential dangers presented by this fluidity and have accepted the need to relate definitions to the historical context in which they emerge. However, many observers continue to pay little regard to such distinctions and, to repeat, concepts such as 'racism' and 'racist' have often become little more than smear terms exploited for political advantage and frequently serve a similar function to 'Commie' and 'Fascist'. However, words must possess a clear meaning: in Dr Johnson's language, they need to be put in their proper place. If the term 'racism' is deployed loosely, without any reference to perceived genetic differences and associated cultural differences, does this mean that a new word is needed for biological-based doctrines and behaviour? The debate on racism is nowhere near its end. In the meantime words and concepts need to be used precisely and accurately if racism, in all its various forms, is ever to be understood.

By concentrating on national developments it becomes possible to question the widespread celebratory vision of Britain as a country characterized by a prevailing spirit of toleration. However, the passing recognition that toleration possesses a relative as well as an absolute dimension nevertheless now encourages a brief consideration of cross-national perspectives. In pursuing this theme the central spotlight hovers on immigrants, refugees and related minorities. The treatment of indigenous groups such as the American Indians, and the responses towards conquered minorities, for example in the form of the various groups who came under German control during the Second World War, fall outside the major focus of this comparative enquiry.

This is not the time or place to mount a comprehensive comparative study. Instead, a limited number of themes can be considered, starting with a reminder that newcomers and minorities in other societies have experienced similar hostility to that which confronted such groups in Britain.

It is possible to locate people in other countries who rank alongside the severely prejudiced personalities who operated in Britain. In France's Third Republic the rabid, unchanging anti-semitism of Edouard Drumont, author of *La France juive* and editor of *La Libre Parole*, can be considered in tandem with that of Joseph Banister. The more sophisticated form of racist opposition expressed towards Russian Polish Jews in 1925–6 by Karl Pearson found its equivalent in America in Madison Grant's anxiety about immigration from southern and eastern Europe which resulted in 1916 in *The Passing of the Great Race*, a work which 'made race the supreme value and repudiated all others inconsistent with it'.[17]

The persistent discrimination encountered by Blacks and Asians in Britain since the Second World War finds a parallel not only in the treatment of guest-workers such as the Turks in Germany, and the former French colonials from North Africa who came to seek their fortune in the bright lights of Paris, but also in the hostility directed in several countries towards Blacks from the Caribbean. The experiences in France of newcomers from Guadaloupe and Martinique and of the Surinamese and Antillean groups in Holland reveal clear similarities with the history of Blacks in Britain.

Immigrants in countries other than Britain have also had to confront collective violence. A number of Italian immigrants were lynched in New Orleans in 1890–1. During the more recent past collective violence has continued to persist. In France North Africans have been vulnerable. In Germany in the 1980s the bulk of such violence has been directed against the Turks, 'the minority within the minority' who have frequently encountered hostility 'even from other foreign nationalities'.[18]

America and Europe, like Britain, also witnessed the emergence of organized opposition. Organizations such as the Scottish Protestant League and the Protestant Action Society, formed in Scotland in the inter-war years, had an earlier counterpart in the American Protective Association which, from its foundation in 1887, took a stand against Catholic influence in America. Other organizational parallels can be identified in the years after 1945. It is well known that present-day Fascist and racial nationalist organizations in Britain, which are hostile to Jews, Blacks, Asians and other groups, are part of a European network with links in countries such as Belgium, France, Italy and Germany. In some cases these contacts also extend to America.

At the level of official policy, State intervention in the shape of immigration control, deportation and internment, was not confined to Britain. Before the 1905 Aliens Act had been placed on the statute-book in Britain, 'a concern for the preservation of the German national character'[19] had resulted in the first attempts in Germany between 1886 and 1890 to expel all alien Poles, and by 1907 a system of identity cards had been instituted to control this immigrant group. Other countries also began to restrict immigration in the years before the First World War. By 1901 Australia had adopted an official White Australia policy: it remained in force until 1973. Canada followed suit in 1910 and maintained this stance until

1962. In 1882 America imposed controls over the arrival of the Chinese. Then, with the increase in entry from southern and eastern Europe, a battery of restrictions began to descend in 1882, reaching a culmination in the 1924 Johnson-Reed Act which related future immigration to national origins and to numbers present in the 1890 census. Basic American immigration law remained tied to this system of ethnic origins until 1965. It is only since this change that Asian, Latin American and south-eastern European groups have been able to increase significantly in size.

In considering the years since the Second World War, the increasingly restrictive immigration policy pursued in Britain from 1962 can be viewed against similar developments in European countries. In France and the Federal Republic of Germany substantial immigration has occurred since 1945. This process created considerable public unease. As a result, in 1973, the Federal Republic imposed controls on the immigration of non-EEC (European Economic Community) nationals. The French Government erected similar restrictions in 1974. Norway, Denmark, Sweden, the Netherlands and Switzerland all followed suit. From the 1970s, therefore, across the face of western and central Europe, migrant workers faced problems of access.

Deportations also occurred in other countries. American officials busied themselves on this account after the First World War as they succumbed to the 'red scare' which after 1917 spread from Russia across the continents. The State in America also showed no compunction regarding the internment of alien minorities in war time. The US Government confined some German nationals during the Second World War but the major drive, from April 1942 onwards, related to the incarceration of Japanese Americans, some of whom had been born in America. This confinement in 'relocation camps' or 'concentration camps', as critics labelled them, can only be described as 'one of the sorrier chapters in American minority-group history'.[20]

In short, the various forms of hostility which place a question mark against the widespread view of Britain as a tolerant country, were to be found in other nations. A close inspection of the history of other societies, and a consideration of Black and Jewish minorities, suggests that at certain times they faced tougher conditions than they

did in Britain, even if it has to be admitted that hostility is difficult
to measure precisely on a 'type of social Richter scale'.

With that caution in mind, it is worth recalling that any Black
person from the Caribbean who entered the American south in the
first half of the present century had to contend with a comprehensive system of 'Jim-Crow' legislation which had no parallel in
Britain. Following the Supreme Court's decision, in the 1896 case
of Plessy *v*. Ferguson, that 'legislation is powerless to eradicate
racial instincts',[21] the weight of official legal opinion supported the
establishment of 'separate but equal' facilities. This legal decision
remained intact until 1954 when, in the case of Brown *v*. the Board
of Education, the Supreme Court reversed its position and pronounced that the 'separate but equal' facilities in American schools
were 'inherently unequal'[22] and constituted a violation of the Four-
teenth Amendment.

In the case of Jews living in other societies, differences can be
traced between the history of Anglo-Jewry and, for example, those
Jews living in the German Empire. It is hard to imagine a political
career in imperial Germany comparable to that of Disraeli's; the
pressure of anti-Jewish sentiment would not have permitted even a
converted Jew to hold such high political office. In France the
fissures created by the Dreyfus case between 1894 and 1906 ran far
deeper than the impact of the Marconi scandal in Britain. Differences in the pre-war world can also be observed if attention
switches towards Russia. Jews in Tsarist Russia remained uneman-
cipated and faced more physical violence there through pogroms
than in any other European society, including Britain. Finally, the
Jews in Germany during the Hitlerite years underwent pressures
which dwarfed those facing Anglo-Jewry at that time. No system
of official controls similar to the 1935 Nuremberg Laws which
'legitimated racist anti-semitism'[23] ever appeared in Britain.

There might be a tendency, in considering material on Blacks in
the United States and Jewish minorities in various European countries, to deploy such detail to perpetuate the image of Britain as a
decent liberal country. This type of response has been apparent in
reviews of two recent books, one on war-time anti-semitism in
Britain and another on the theme of political intolerance in British
society. However, attempts to treat hostility towards immigrants,

refugees and minorities as marginal or essentially alien to British history or to dismiss its manifestation as insignificant, need to explain away the persistent corpus of evidence on hostility which has already been unearthed. Any celebratory view of Britain can also be severely challenged if one's horizons are raised to the Greater Britain beyond the seas. Incidents such as Morant Bay, Jamaica in 1865, Amritsar in 1919, and lesser-known episodes such as Dinshawi in Egypt in 1906 and Hola Camp, Kenya in 1959, provide convincing testimony on this source. 'If only you could see', wrote Lawrence Durrell to Richard Aldington, 'the behaviour of the Cyprus Police, Malaya and Palestine police, you would be scared at the very strong strain of brutish Fascism the British have in their subconscious'.[24] Testimony on the brutalizing British in the Empire is not confined to such violent incidents. The merciless exploitation of Indian workers, Briain's largest proletariat in the days of the Raj, provides further evidence.

These observations are leading to a point at which a number of emphases need to be made. First, the potential for expressions of hostility towards immigrants, refugees and minorities whether in the form of attitudes or actions, towards individuals or entire groups, resides in all societies, including decent liberal democracies. Second, in considering such opposition, due care should be taken at all times to guard against attempts to erect a rigid 'good', 'better', 'best' ordering of countries. The primary task is to understand such hostility. This exercise involves identifying the specific historical and immediate issues which influenced the responses towards particular groups at specific times. In concrete terms, in spite of the difficulties they faced between 1939 and 1945, Jewish refugees in Britain encountered less trauma than similar Jewish groups in France during these years. In accounting for this difference a moralistic explanation which works to the advantage of Britain is inadequate. It is more important to recognize that pressures resulting from the German occupation of France gave a new propulsion to the French tradition of anti-semitism, in the face of which, alien Jews, born outside France, became especially exposed. Britain was spared the influences of any such occupation. It is in pursuing such arguments that a closer understanding can be gained of why, during the same chronological period, experiences varied across national boundaries. Very little attempt has been made by historians to engage in such comparative analysis. There is certainly nothing on Europe comparable to George Frederickson's *White Supremacy*, an arresting comparative study of the southern states of the USA and South Africa.

This is the point at which to return to our main theme and our starting point. Throughout the years from 1871 there is abundant evidence of the hostile attitudes and treatment which immigrants, refugees and related minorities have endured in Britain, but it would be an error, nevertheless, to portray Britain as a country in which these groups faced universal and unremitting hostility. The diversity and complexity of responses needs to be fully recognized. However, hostility cannot be wiped away as an insignificant smear of grime on the country's bright reputation. Opposition has emerged at both popular and official levels. In short, the problems confronting Blacks and Asians in the 1980s need to be placed alongside the experiences of other groups whose presence bears witness to a continual tradition of immigration into Britain. These cumulative experiences call into question those observations which identify 'a moral trans-historical source' of toleration in British society and dilate upon 'the virtues of Britain, and the qualities of Britons true'.[25] These emphases are among the most distorting celebratory myths in recent British history and act as a stumbling-block against any attempt to understand and combat the various forms of hostility experienced by immigrants, refugees and minorities in Britain.

Notes

I. Contemporary issues

1 E. J. B. Rose, ed., *Colour and Citizenship* (London, 1969), p. 587, but see D. Lawrence, 'How prejudiced are we?', *Race Today*, vol. 1 (October 1969), pp. 174–6.
2 S. Castles and G. Kosack, *Immigrant Workers and Class Structure in Western Europe* (London, 1973), p. 431.
3 R. Jowell and C. Airey, eds, *British Social Attitudes. The 1984 Report* (Aldershot, 1984), pp. 121, 125.
4 *The Times*, 1 April 1988.
5 V. Bevan, *The Development of British Immigration Law* (London, 1986), p. 83.
6 *Parliamentary Debates*, (Commons), vol. 122 (1988), col. 779.
7 D. Murphy, *Tales from Two Cities. Travel of Another Sort* (London, 1987), p. 69.
8 *Parliamentary Debates* (Commons), vol. 138 (1988), col. 422.
9 *Fifth Report from the Home Affairs Committee. Racial Disadvantage*, HC424–1 (London, 1981), p. lxxi.
10 *Runnymede Trust Bulletin*, no. 203 (May, 1987), pp. 2–3.
11 *Sunday Telegraph*, 6 August 1972.
12 Z. Layton-Henry and P. B. Rich, eds, *Race, Government and Politics in Britain* (London, 1986), p. 95.
13 *Sunday Telegraph*, 3 August 1986.
14 P. Worsthorne on *Panorama*, BBC1 TV, 11 April 1988.

II. A tolerant country?

1 H. Butterfield, *The Englishman and his History* (Cambridge, 1944), p. 1.
2 G. Orwell, *The Lion and the Unicorn* (Harmondsworth, 1982 edn), p. 141.
3 M. Harmon, ed., *Fenians and Fenianism* (Dublin, 1970), p. 48.
4 R. Benewick, *The Fascist Movement in Britain* (London, 1972), p. 10.

5 *Scotsman*, 15 July 1935.

6 *Parliamentary Debates* (Commons), vol. 594 (1958–9), col. 418.

7 J. Henderson, 'Race Relations in Britain', in *Coloured Immigrants in Britain*, ed. J. A. G. Griffith, et al., (London, 1960), p. 47.

8 Letter, John Smyth to Reg Deering of Lambeth Inter-Racial Council, 27 January 1964.

9 *Immigration from the Commonwealth*, Cmnd 2739 (1965), p. 18.

10 *Sunday Telegraph*, 3 August 1986.

11 Parliamentary Debates (Commons), vol. 162 (1906), col. 1357.

12 M. Beerbohm, *Fifty Caricatures* (London, 1913), no. 47.

13 *Royal Commission on Alien Immigration*, British Parliamentary Papers, IX (1903), pp. 286, 293.

14 J. L. Silver in *Eastern Post and City Chronicle*, 2 November 1901.

15 *John Bull*, 15 May 1915.

16 G. T. Zytaruk and J. T. Boulton, eds, *The Letters of D. H. Lawrence*, vol. 11, June 1913–October 1916 (Cambridge, 1981), p. 340.

17 *The Times*, 7 October 1914.

18 *Parliamentary Debates* (Commons), vol. 114 (1919), col. 2799.

19 *ibid.*, col. 2765.

20 C. Holmes, *John Bull's Island. Immigration and British Society 1871–1971* (London, 1988), p. 114.

21 P. Fryer, *Staying Power. The History of Black People in Britain* (London, 1984), p. 301.

22 K. O'Connor, *The Irish in Britain* (Dublin, 1974), p. 46.

23 A. J. Sherman, *Island Refuge. Britain and Refugees from the Third Reich 1933–1939* (London, 1973), p. 267.

24 *Jewish Chronicle*, 9 January 1931.

25 M. Muggeridge, *The Thirties, 1930–1940* (London, 1940), p. 243.

26 K. Nkrumah, *The Autobiography of Kwame Nkrumah* (Edinburgh, 1957), p. 49.

27 P. B. Rich, 'Philanthropic Racism in Britain. The Anti-Slavery Society and Half-Caste Children between the Wars', *Immigrants and Minorities*, vol. 3 (1984), pp. 69–88. See also his *Race and Empire* (Cambridge, 1986), Ch. 5.

28 K. Little, *Negroes in Britain. A Study of Racial Relations in English Society* (London, 1948), p. 60.

29 N. Evans, 'Regulating the Reserve Army. Arabs, Blacks and the Local State in Cardiff 1919–45', *Immigrants and Minorities*, vol. 4 (1985), p. 80.

30 Mass Observation File Report 107: Feeling about Aliens, 14 May 1940.

31 M. Kochan, *Britain's Internees in the Second World War* (London, 1983), Ch. 4.

32 B. Wasserstein, *Britain and the Jews of Europe 1939–1945* (Oxford, 1979), pp. 99, 101.

33 S. Cronin, *Irish Nationalism* (Dublin, 1980), p. 161.

34 Quoted in M. Gilbert, *Winston S. Churchill*, vol. 6, 'Finest Hour 1939–1945' (Oxford, 1983), p. 71.

35 PRO INF 1/264/194, 10 June 1940.

36 PRO INF 1/292/279, 7–14 March 1944.

37 A. Watson, *West Indian Workers in Great Britain* (London, 1942), p. 14 and PRO CO 874/48.

38 E. J. Hobsbawm, 'Are we entering a New Era of Anti-Semitism?', *New Society*, 11 December 1980, p. 503.

39 S. Patterson, 'The Poles: An Exile Community in Britain', in *Between Two Cultures*, ed. J. L. Watson (Oxford, 1977), p. 240.

40 TUC, *Annual Report* (London, 1946), p. 357.

41 J. Zubrzycki, *Polish Immigrants in Britain. A Study of Adjustment* (The Hague, 1956), p. 82.

42 *ibid.*

43 J. A. Tannahill, *European Volunteer Workers in Britain* (Manchester, 1958), p. 70.

44 J. A. Jackson, *The Irish in Britain* (London, 1963), pp. 63, 108, 177.

45 O'Connor, *op. cit.*, p. 121.

46 PRO PREM 8/827.

47 *Parliamentary Debates* (Commons), vol. 451 (1947–8), col. 1851.

48 PRO LAB 8/1516.

49 PRO CAB 128/38, 19 June 1950.

50 PRO CAB 129/65, memo of 3 February 1954.

51 R. Crossman, *The Diaries of a Cabinet Minister*, vol. 1, Minister of Housing 1964–66 (London, 1975), p. 149.

52 *ibid.*

53 *Patterns of Prejudice*, vol. 1 (March–April 1967), p. 23; see also C. Husbands, *Racial Exclusionism and the City. The Urban Support of the National Front* (London, 1983).

54 B. Smithies and P. Fiddick, eds, *Enoch Powell on Immigration* (London, 1969), p. 36.

55 *ibid.*, p. 43; see also *The Times*, 19 April 1988.

56 *Parliamentary Debates* (Commons), vol. 759 (1967–68), col. 1299.

57 The Runnymede Trust and Radical Statistics Race Group, *Britain's Black Population* (London, 1980), p. 39.

58 Fryer, *op. cit.*, p. 389; H. V. Carby, 'Schooling in Babylon', in *The Empire Strikes Back*, ed. Centre for Contemporary Cultural Studies (London, 1982), pp. 183–211.

III. Hostility explored

1 *Sunday Telegraph*, 24 April 1988.

2 *The Times*, 17 August 1982 (letters).

3 M. Banton, *Racial Minorities* (London, 1973), p. 103.

4 N. Ackerman and M. Jahoda, *Antisemitism and Emotional Disorder. A Psychoanalytic Interpretation* (New York, 1950), pp. 1–2.

5 J.-P. Sartre, *Portrait of the Anti-Semite* (London, 1948), p. 10.

6 Paragraph taken from J. Banister, *England under the Jews* (London, 1907), pp. 81, 21–2.

7 *ibid.*, 61.

8 Soskice Papers. House of Lords, BA/1, letter of 25 January 1904.

9 J. Higham, 'Anti-Semitism in the Gilded Age', *Mississippi Valley Historical Review*, vol. 43 (1956–7), p. 563.

10 Banister, *op. cit.*, pp. 77–80.

11 *ibid.*, pp. 1–2.

12 H. J. Eysenck, 'The Psychology of Anti-Semitism', in H. J. Eysenck, *Uses and Abuses of Psychology* (Harmondsworth, 1960), p. 268.

13 S. Bruce, *No Pope of Rome. Militant Protestantism in Modern Scotland* (Edinburgh, 1985), p. 62.

14 *ibid.*, p. 60.

15 *ibid.*, p. 62.

16 G. Plekhanov, *The Materialist Conception of History* (New York, 1964 edn), p. 16.

17 J. Higham, *Strangers in the Land. Patterns of American Nativism 1860–1925* (New York, 1965), p. 402.

18 Centre for Contemporary Cultural Studies, *op. cit.*, p. 182.

19 J. D. Chambers, *The Workshop of the World* (Oxford, 1968).

20 V. G. Kiernan, *The Lords of Human Kind* (Harmondsworth, 1972).

21 C. Hill, *God's Englishman. Oliver Cromwell and the English Revolution* (London, 1970), p. 113.

22 Bradford Heritage Recording Unit, Tape M006/01/22.

23 M. D. Biddiss, 'Racial Ideas and the Politics of Prejudice 1850–1914', *Historical Journal*, vol. 15 (1972), p. 572.

24 V. G. Kiernan, 'Britons Old and New', in *Immigrants and Minorities in British Society*, ed. C. Holmes (London, 1978), p. 54.

25 M. Banton, *Racial and Ethnic Competition* (Cambridge, 1983), p. 290.

26 A. Lee, 'Aspects of the Working-Class Response to the Jews in Britain, 1880–1914', in *Hosts, Immigrants and Minorities. Historical Responses to Newcomers in British Society 1870–1914*, ed. K. Lunn (Folkestone, 1980), p. 123.

27 *ibid.*, p. 124.

28 A. Marshall, *Principles of Economics* (8th edn, London, 1925), p. 761, n. 1.

29 S. Gilley, 'English Attitudes to the Irish in England 1789–1900', in Holmes, ed., *op. cit.*, p. 81.

30 *ibid.*, p. 85.

31 P. Worsthorne, in Lord Elton, *The Unarmed Invasion. A Survey of*

Afro-Asian Immigration (London, 1965), p. 85.

32 *The Times*, 22 February 1990.

33 *Sunday Telegraph*, 19 February 1989.

34 *The Times*, 25 March 1935; *Blackshirt*, 29 March 1935, reporting a speech at the Albert Hall.

35 Quoted in B. Gainer, *The Alien Invasion. The Origins of the Aliens Act of 1905* (London, 1972), p. 12.

36 *Royal Commission on Alien Immigration*, p. 298.

37 *Parliamentary Debates* (Commons), vol. 101 (1902), col. 1274.

38 *ibid.*, vol. 532 (1953–4), col. 821.

39 B. Smithies and P. Fiddick, eds, *Enoch Powell on Immigration* (London, 1969), p. 68.

40 *Daily Mail*, 31 January 1978.

41 R. Glass in *The Times*, 16 February 1968; see also S. Allen, *New Minorities. Old Conflicts* (New York, 1971), pp. 59–60.

42 D. Murphy, *Tales from Two Cities. Travel of Another Sort* (London, 1987), p. 67.

43 K. Lunn, 'Reactions to Lithuanian and Polish Immigrants in the Lanarkshire Coalfield 1880–1914', in Lunn, ed., *op. cit.*, p. 323.

44 R. Fevre, *Cheap Labour and Racial Discrimination* (Aldershot, 1984), p. 64.

45 C. Holmes, *Anti-Semitism in British Society 1876–1939* (London, 1979), p. 16.

46 J. Tannahill, *European Volunteer Workers in Britain* (Manchester, 1958).

47 *Observer*, Supplement, 19 December 1971.

48 N. Evans, 'The South Wales Race Riots of 1919', *Llafur*, vol. 3 (1980), p. 14.

49 G. W. Allport, *The Nature of Prejudice* (Reading, Mass., 1954), p. 27.

50 Smithies and Fiddick, *op. cit.*, p. 73.

51 *Sunday Telegraph*, 13 August 1989 and letters 20 August 1989.

52 K. Sword, '"Their Prospects will not be Bright". British Responses to the Problem of Polish "Recalcitrants" 1946–49', *Journal of Contemporary History*, vol. 21 (1986), pp. 363–90.

53 T. Acton, *Gypsy Politics and Social Change* (London, 1974), p. 195.

54 J. Okely, *Changing Cultures. The Traveller Gypsies* (Cambridge, 1983), p. 113.

55 R. R. James, ed., *Chips. The Diaries of Sir Henry Channon* (London, 1967), p. 120.

56 Mass Observation Archive, Dr 2683 (March 1943).

57 Higham, 'Anti-Semitism', p. 563.

58 J. A. Jackson, *The Irish in Britain* (London, 1963), p. 108.

59 Rich, *Immigrants and Minorities*, pp. 69–88.

60 L. Dinnerstein, R. Nichols and D. M. Reimers, *Natives and*

Strangers. Ethnic Groups and the Building of America (New York, 1979), p. 295.

61 B. Williams, 'The Anti-Semitism of Tolerance. Middle-Class Manchester and the Jews 1870–1900', in *City, Class and Culture. Studies of Social Policy and Cultural Production in Victorian Manchester*, ed. A. J. Kidd and K. W. Roberts (Manchester, 1985), p. 94.

62 Quoted in M. Banton, 'Social Acceptance and Rejection', in *Colour in Britain*, ed. R. Hooper (London, 1965), p. 115.

IV Conclusion

1 J. Geipel, *The Europeans. An Ethnohistorical Survey* (London, 1969), pp. 163–4.

2 E. Burke, *Reflections on the Revolution in France* (London, 1969 edn), p.82.

3 C. Holmes, 'Immigration', in *Population and Society in Great Britain 1850–1950*, ed. T. Barker and M. Drake (London, 1982), p. 178.

4 N. Frangopulo, *Rich Inheritance. A Guide to the History of Manchester* (Manchester, 1962), p. 110.

5 I. Mikardo, 'Peace with a Cockney Accent', *Sunday Telegraph Magazine*, 11 April 1982.

6 P. Kropotkin, *Memoirs of a Revolutionist* (London, 1899), vol. 2, p. 180.

7 *Bradford Telegraph and Argus*, 31 October 1984.

8 *Parliamentary Debates* (Lords), vol. 494 (1988), col. 376.

9 H. Arendt, *The Origins of Totalitarianism* (London, 1958), p. ix.

10 H. J. Ehrlich, *The Social Psychology of Prejudice* (New York, 1973), pp. 3–4.

11 Diane Abbott, quoted in *Sunday Times*, 10 April 1988.

12 Quoted in *Daily Express*, 23 April 1988.

13 R. Moore, *Racism and Black Resistance* (London, 1975), p. 29.

14 M. D. Biddiss, 'Toward a History of European Racism', *Ethnic and Racial Studies*, vol. 2 (1979), p. 508. See also his 'Myths of the Blood', *Patterns of Prejudice*, vol. 9 (1975), pp. 11–19.

15 J. Rex, *Race Relations in Sociological Theory* (London, 1970), pp. 157, 159.

16 *Guardian*, 20 March 1990.

17 J. Higham, *Strangers in the Land. Patterns of American Nativism 1860–1925* (New York, 1965), p. 157.

18 S. Castles, et al., *Here for Good. Western Europe's New Ethnic Minorities* (London, 1984), p. 100.

19 J. M. Zuckerman, 'Aliens in the German *Rechtstaat*. The Constitutional Rights of Aliens in Germany 1871–1975', PhD Thesis, University of Nebraska at Lincoln, 1979, p. 54.

20 L. Dinnerstein, R. Nichols and D. M. Reimers, *Natives and*

Strangers. Ethnic Groups and the Building of America (New York, 1979), p. 246.

21 C. Vann Woodward, *The Strange Career of Jim Crow* (New York, 1966), p. 71.

22 *ibid.*, p. 147.

23 L. Dawidowicz, *The War against the Jews 1933–45* (Harmondsworth, 1977), p. 95.

24 I. MacNiven and H. T. Moore, eds., *Literary Lifelines* (London, 1981), p. 54.

25 C. Holmes, 'Anti-Semitism and the BUF', in *British Fascism*, ed. K. Lunn and R. C. Thurlow (London, 1980), pp. 129–30.

Select bibliography

BOOKS

Acton, T., *Gypsy Politics and Social Change*, London, 1974
Allport, G. W., *The Nature of Prejudice*, Reading, Mass., 1954
Anwar, M., *The Myth of Return. Pakistanis in Britain*, London, 1979
Ashton, R., *Little Germany. Exile and Asylum in Victorian England*, Oxford, 1986
Banton, M., *The Coloured Quarter*, London, 1955
——, *Race Relations*, London, 1967
——, *Racial and Ethnic Competition*, Cambridge, 1983
Bethlehem, D., *A Social Psychology of Prejudice*, London, 1985
Bevan, V., *The Development of British Immigration Law*, London, 1986
Bird, J. C., *Control of Enemy Alien Civilians in Great Britain, 1914–1918*, New York and London, 1986
Brown, C., *Black and White Britain. The Third PSI Survey*, London, 1984
Centre for Contemporary Cultural Studies, *The Empire Strikes Back*, London, 1982
Ehrlich, H. J., *The Social Psychology of Prejudice*, New York, 1973
Fishman, W. J., *The Streets of East London*, London, 1979
Foot, P., *Immigration and Race in British Politics*, Harmondsworth, 1965
Fryer, P., *Staying Power. The History of Black People in Britain*, London, 1984
Gallagher, T., *Edinburgh Divided. John Cormack and No Popery in the 1930s*, Edinburgh, 1987
——, *Glasgow. The Uneasy Truce*, Manchester, 1987
Garrard, J. A., *The English and Immigration. A Comparative Study of the Jewish Influx 1880–1910*, London, 1971
Gartner, L., *The Jewish Immigrant in England 1870–1914*, Detroit, 1960 and London, 1973
Gilroy, P., *There ain't no Black in the Union Jack*, London, 1987
Hirschfeld, G., ed., *Exile in Great Britain. Refugees from Hitler's Germany*, Leamington Spa, 1984
Holmes, C., ed., *Immigrants and Minorities in British Society*, London, 1978

Select bibliography

——, *Anti-Semitism in British Society 1876–1939*, London 1979

——, *John Bull's Island. Immigration and British Society 1871–1971*, London, 1988

Hornsby-Smith, M., *Roman Catholics in England. Studies in Social Structure since the Second World War*, Cambridge, 1987

Jackson, J. A., *The Irish in Britain*, London, 1963

Kushner, T., *The Persistence of Prejudice. Anti-Semitism in British Society during the Second World War*, Manchester 1989

Kushner T., and Lunn, K., eds, *Traditions of Intolerance*, Manchester 1989

Lafitte, F., *The Internment of Aliens*, Harmondsworth, 1940 and London, 1988

Layton-Henry, Z., and Rich, P. B., eds, *Race, Government and Politics in Britain*, London, 1986

Little, K., *Negroes in Britain. A Study of Racial Relations in English Society*, London, 1948 and 1972

Lunn, K., ed., *Hosts, Immigrants and Minorities. Historical Responses to Newcomers in British Society 1870–1914*, Folkstone, 1980

——, *Race and Labour in Twentieth-Century Britain*, London, 1985

Mayall, D., *Gypsy-Travellers in Nineteenth-Century Society*, Cambridge, 1988

Miles, R., *Racism and Migrant Labour*, London, 1982

——, *Racism*, London, 1989

Murphy, D., *Tales from Two Cities. Travel of Another Sort*, London, 1987

Neal, F., *Sectarian Violence. The Liverpool Experience 1819–1914. An Aspect of Anglo-Irish History*, Manchester, 1988

O'Connor, K., *The Irish in Britain*, Dublin, 1974

Pollins, H., *Economic History of the Jews in England*, London and Toronto, 1982

Porter, B., *The Refugee Question in Mid-Victorian Politics*, Cambridge, 1979

Ramdin, R., *The Making of the Black Working Class in Britain*, Aldershot, 1987

Rex, J., *Race, Colonialism and the City*, London, 1973

Rex, J., and Moore, R., *Race, Community and Conflict. A Study of Sparkbrook*, London, 1967

Rex, J., and Tomlinson, S., *Colonial Immigrants in a British City*, London, 1979

Rich, P. B., *Race and Empire*, Cambridge, 1986

Rose, E. J. B., ed., *Colour and Citizenship*, London, 1969

Sherwood, M., *Many Struggles. West Indian Workers and Service Personnel in Britain 1939–45*, London, 1985

Sivanandan, A., *A Different Hunger. Writings on Black Resistance*, London, 1983

Smith, D. J., *The Facts of Racial Disadvantage*, London, 1976

Smith, G., *When Jim Crow met John Bull. Black American Soldiers in World War II Britain*, London, 1987

Smithies, B., and Fiddick, P., eds, *Enoch Powell on Immigration*, London, 1969

Solomos, J., *Race and Racism in Contemporary Britain*, London, 1989

Sponza, L., *Italian Immigrants in Nineteenth-Century Britain. Realities and Images*, Leicester, 1988

Stone, J., *Racial Conflict in Contemporary Society*, London, 1985

Swift, R., and Gilley, S., eds, *The Irish in the Victorian City*, London, 1985

——, *The Irish in Britain 1815–1939*, London, 1989

Sword, K., et al., *The Formation of the Polish Community in Great Britain 1939–50*, London, 1989

Tannahill, J. A., *European Volunteer Workers in Britain*, Manchester, 1958

Visram, R., *Ayahs, Lascars and Princes. Indians in Britain 1700–1947*, London, 1986

Waller, P. J., *Democracy and Sectarianism. A Political and Social History of Liverpool 1868–1939*, Liverpool, 1981

Walvin, J., *Passage to Britain*, Harmondsworth, 1984

Wasserstein, B., *Britain and the Jews of Europe 1939–1945*, Oxford, 1979

Watson, J. L., ed., *Between Two Cultures*, Oxford, 1977

Zubrzycki, J., *Polish Immigrants in Britain. A Study of Adjustment*, The Hague, 1956

ARTICLES AND CONTRIBUTIONS TO BOOKS

Anderson, G. L., 'German Clerks in England 1870–1914. Another Aspect of the Great Depression Debate', in *Hosts, Immigrants and Minorities. Historical Responses to Newcomers in British Society 1870–1914*, ed. K. Lunn, Folkstone, 1980

Banton, M., 'The Idiom of Race. A Critique of Presentism', *Research in Racial and Ethnic Relations*, vol. 2, 1980

Berridge, V., 'East End Opium Dens and Narcotic Use in Britain', *London Journal*, vol. 4, 1978

Biddiss, M. D., 'Myths of the Blood', *Patterns of Prejudice*, vol. 9, 1975

Cesarani, D., 'Anti-Alienism in England after the First World War', *Immigrants and Minorities*, vol. 6, 1987

Dollard, J., 'Hostility and Fear in Social Life', *Social Forces*, vol. 17, 1938

Evans, N., 'The South Wales Race Riots of 1919', *Llafur*, vol. 3, 1980

——, 'Regulating the Reserve Army. Arabs, Blacks and the Local State in Cardiff 1919–45', *Immigrants and Minorities*, vol. 4, 1985

Grimshaw, A. D., 'Relationships among Prejudice, Discrimination,

Social Tension and Social Violence', *Journal of Intergroup Relations*, vol. 2, 1961

Higham, J., 'Anti-Semitism in the Gilded Age', *Mississippi Valley Historical Review*, vol. 43, 1956–7

Hobsbawm, E. J., 'Are we entering a New Era of Anti-Semitism?', *New Society*, 11 December 1980

Hoch, P. K., 'The Reception of Central European Refugee Physicists of the 1930s. USSR, UK, USA', *Annals of Science*, vol. 40, 1983

Holmes, C., 'The German Gypsy Question in Britain 1904–06', *Journal of the Gypsy Lore Society*, vol. 1, 1978

——, 'The Tredegar Riots of 1911. Anti-Jewish Disturbances in South Wales', *Welsh History Review*, vol. 11, 1982

Husbands, C., 'East End Racism 1900–1980. Continuities in Vigilantist and Extreme Right-Wing Political Behaviour', *London Journal*, vol. 8, 1982

Kee, R., 'Is there a British Colour Bar?', *Picture Post*, 2 July 1949

Kiernan, V. G., 'Britons Old and New', in *Immigrants and Minorities in British Society*, ed. C. Holmes, London, 1978

Kushner, T., 'Asylum or Servitude? Refugee Domestics in Britain 1933–1945', *Bulletin of the Society for the Study of Labour History*, vol. 53, 1988

Lee, A., 'Aspects of the Working-Class Response to the Jews in Britain 1880–1914', in *Hosts, Immigrants and Minorities. Historical Responses to Newcomers in British Society 1870–1914*, ed. K. Lunn, Folkstone, 1980

Leech, K., '"Diverse Reports" and the Meaning of "Racism"', *Race and Class*, vol. 28, 1986

May, J. P., 'The Chinese in Britain 1860–1914', in *Immigrants and Minorities in British Society*, ed. C. Holmes, London, 1978

Ó Tuathaigh, M. A. G., 'The Irish in Nineteenth-Century Britain. Problems of Integration', *Transactions of the Royal Historical Society*, vol. 31, 1981

Oakley, R., 'The Control of Cypriot Migration to Britain between the Wars', *Immigrants and Minorities*, vol. 6, 1987

Panayi, P., 'The Lancashire Anti-German Riots of May 1915', *Manchester Region History Review*, vol. 11, Autumn/Winter 1988–9

Patterson, S., 'The Poles: An Exile Community in Britain', in *Between Two Cultures*, ed. J. L. Watson, Oxford, 1977

Peach, C., 'The Growth and Distribution of the Black Population in Britain 1945–1980', in *Demography of Immigrants and Minority Groups in the United Kingdom*, ed. D. A. Coleman, London, 1982

Porter, B., '"Bureau and Barrack": Early Victorian Attitudes towards the Continent', *Victorian Studies*, vol. 27, 1984

Rich, P. B., 'Philanthropic Racism in Britain. The Anti-Slavery Society and Half-Caste Children between the Wars', *Immigrants and Minorities*, vol. 3, 1984

Rodgers, M., 'The Anglo-Russian Military Convention and the Lithuanian Immigrant Community in Lanarkshire, Scotland 1914–20', *Immigrants and Minorities*, vol. 1, 1982

Searle, C., 'Your Daily Dose. Racism and the *Sun*', *Race and Class*, vol. 29, 1987

Sivanandan, A., 'RAT and the Degradation of the Black Struggle', *Race and Class*, vol. 26, 1985

Smith, A., 'War and Ethnicity. The Role of Warfare in the Formation, Self-Images and Cohesion of Ethnic Communities', *Ethnic and Racial Studies*, vol. 4, 1981

Sword, K., '"Their Prospects will not be Bright". British Responses to the Problem of Polish "Recalcitrants" 1946–49', *Journal of Contemporary History*, vol. 21, 1986

Tajfel, H., 'Stereotypes', *Race*, vol. 5, 1963

Williams, B., 'The Anti-Semitism of Tolerance. Middle-Class Manchester and the Jews 1870–1900', in *City, Class and Culture. Studies of Social Policy and Cultural Production in Victorian Manchester*, ed. A. J. Kidd and K. W. Roberts, Manchester, 1985

Zawadzki, B., 'Limitations of the Scapegoat Theory of Prejudice', *Journal of Abnormal and Social Psychology*, vol. 43, 1948

REPORTS

Loosen the Shackles. First Report of the Liverpool 8 Inquiry into Race Relations in Liverpool, London, 1989

Royal Commission on Alien Immigration, British Parliamentary Papers, IX, London, 1903

The Brixton Disorders 10–12 April 1981, Cmnd 8427, London, 1981

War Crimes. Report of the War Crimes Enquiry, Cm. 744, London, 1989

Index